INFORMATION TECHNOLOGY WORKSHOP IN MATLAB

AUTHOR

Dr. Hari Prabhat Gupta

Assistant Professor, IIT (BHU) Varanasi

REVIEWER

Dr. Sandeep Kumar

Associate Professor,

Indian Institute of Technology, Roorkee

KHANNA BOOK PUBLISHING CO. (P) Ltd.

4C/4344, Ansari Road, Darya Ganj, New Delhi, India

All India Council for Technical Education

Nelson Mandela Marg, Vasant Kunj, New Delhi, India

Dear Readers,

To prevent the piracy, this book is secured with HIGH SECURITY HOLOGRAM on the front title cover. In case you don't find the hologram on the front cover title, please write us to at contact@khannabooks.com or whatsapp us at +91-99109 09320 and avail special gift voucher for yourself.

Specimen of Hologram on front Cover title:

Moreover, there is a SPECIAL DISCOUNT COUPON for you with EVERY HOLOGRAM.

How to avail this SPECIAL DISCOUNT:

Step 1: Scratch the hologram
Step 2: Under the scratch area, your "coupon code" is available
Step 3: Logon to www.khannabooks.com
Step 4: Use your "coupon code" in the shopping cart and get your copy at a special discount
Step 5: Enjoy your reading!

ISBN: 978-93-5538-968-8
Book Code: UG405EN

Information Technology Workshop in Matlab

by Dr. Hari Prabhat Gupta

First Edition: 2026

Originally Published by:
All India Council for Technical Education, Ministry of Education, GOI

Exclusively Published & Distributed by:
Khanna Book Publishing Co. (P) Ltd.
4C/4344, Ansari Road, Daryaganj,
New Delhi (INDIA)

Visit us at: **www.khannabooks.com**
Write us at: **contact@khannabooks.com**

To view complete list of books, Please scan the QR Code: KPH

Printed in Bharat.

प्रो. म. जगदीश कुमार
अध्यक्ष
Prof. M. Jagadesh Kumar
Chairman

सत्यमेव जयते

आज़ादी का अमृत महोत्सव

अखिल भारतीय तकनीकी शिक्षा परिषद्
(भारत सरकार का एक सांविधिक निकाय)
(शिक्षा मंत्रालय, भारत सरकार)
नेल्सन मंडेला मार्ग, वसंत कुंज, नई दिल्ली-110070
दूरभाष : 011-26131498
ई-मेल : chairman@aicte-india.org

ALL INDIA COUNCIL FOR TECHNICAL EDUCATION
(A STATUTORY BODY OF THE GOVT. OF INDIA)
(Ministry of Education, Govt. of India)
Nelson Mandela Marg, Vasant Kunj, New Delhi-110070
Phone : 011-26131498
E-mail : chairman@aicte-india.org

FOREWORD

Engineers are the backbone of the modern society. It is through them that engineering marvels have happened and improved quality of life across the world. They have driven humanity towards greater heights in a more evolved and unprecedented manner.

The All India Council for Technical Education (AICTE), led from the front and assisted students, faculty & institutions in every possible manner towards the strengthening of the technical education in the country. AICTE is always working towards promoting quality Technical Education to make India a modern developed nation with the integration of modern knowledge & traditional knowledge for the welfare of mankind.

An array of initiatives have been taken by AICTE in last decade which have been accelerate now by the National Education Policy (NEP) 2020. The implementation of NEP under the visionary leadership of Hon'ble Prime Minister of India envisages the provision for education in regional languages to all, thereby ensuring that every graduate becomes competent enough and is in a position to contribute towards the national growth and development through innovation & entrepreneurship.

One of the spheres where AICTE had been relentlessly working since 2021-22 is providing high quality books prepared and translated by eminent educators in various Indian languages to its engineering students at Under Graduate & Diploma level. For the second year students, AICTE has identified 87 books at Under Graduate and Diploma Level courses, for translation in 12 Indian languages - Hindi, Tamil, Gujarati, Odia, Bengali, Kannada, Urdu, Punjabi, Telugu, Marathi, Assamese & Malayalam. In addition to the English medium, the 1044 books in different Indian Languages are going to support to engineering students to learn in their mother tongue. Currently, there are 39 institutions in 11 states offering courses in Indian languages in 7 disciplines like Biomedical Engineering, Civil Engineering, Computer Science & Engineering, Electrical Engineering, Electronics & Communication Engineering, Information Technology Engineering & Mechanical Engineering, Architecture, and Interior Designing. This will become possible due to active involvement and support of universities/institutions in different states.

On behalf of AICTE, I express sincere gratitude to all distinguished authors, reviewers and translators from different IITs, NITs and other institutions for their admirable contribution in a very short span of time.

AICTE is confident that these out comes based books with their rich content will help technical students master the subjects with factor comprehension and greater ease.

(Prof. M. Jagadesh Kumar)

ABOUT THE AUTHOR

Hari Prabhat Gupta is working as faculty in the Department of Computer Science and Engineering, Indian Institute of Technology (BHU) Varanasi. Previously, Hari was a Technical Lead in Samsung R&D Bangalore, India. Hari received his Ph.D. and M.Tech. degrees in Computer Science and Engineering from Indian Institute of Technology Guwahati; and his B.E. degree in Computer Engineering from Govt. Engineering College Ajmer, India. Hari has elevated to the grade of Senior Member of IEEE in June 2020 based on his significant contributions to the profession. Hari successfully organized short-term courses under Quality Improvement Programme, courses under Global Initiative of Academic Networks (GIAN), VRITIKA training program, and other continuing education programs in the domain of smart sensing, machine learning, and wireless sensing. Hari has published three Indian patents and more than 150 research papers in journals and conferences. Hari was awarded TCS research fellowship, Samsung spot awards, and best teacher awards. Hari has finished various research projects sponsored by different government and private organizations.

ACKNOWLEDGEMENTS

The author is grateful to AICTE for their meticulous planning and execution to publish the technical book for Engineering and Technology students. I sincerely acknowledge the valuable contributions of the reviewer of the book Prof. Sandeep Kumar, for making it students' friendly and giving a better shape in an artistic manner. This book is an outcome of various suggestions of AICTE members, experts and authors who shared their opinion and thoughts to further develop the engineering education in our country. It is also with great honour that we state that this book is aligned to the AICTE Model Curriculum and in line with the guidelines of NEP-2020. Towards promoting education in regional languages, this book is being translated in scheduled Indian regional languages. Acknowledgements are due to the contributors and different workers in this field whose published books, review articles, papers, photographs, footnotes, references and other valuable information enriched us at thetime of writing the book. I like to express my sincere thanks to Dr. Rahul Bansal who helped me to write this book. Dr. Bansal worked with me from the beginning of the book and especially gave suggestions for writing the examples, questionnaire, and experiments. Finally, I thank my Mother- Prabhat Gupta and my wife—Tanima Dutta—for their love and support while I prepared this book. The patience and encouragement of my family made this project possible. I affectionately dedicate this book to them.

Hari Prabhat Gupta

Indian Institute of Technology (BHU) Varanasi, India

PREFACE

The book entitled Information Technology (IT) Workshop is a result of our vast experience of teaching and research in programming languages. This book initiates with the introduction to IT workshop, which covers the different domains of IT workshop. It then explores the one of the most widely used programming language i.e. MATLAB. Main purpose of this book is to help students and researchers to understand and apply the MATLAB programming language to different engineering applications.

This book starts with the basic concepts of MATLAB programming and describes the applications of each concept in detail. The major content of the book consists of the topics suggested by AICTE and described in a systematic and simple way. This book consists of the numerous solved and unsolved problems which will help the students to develop their critical thinking and logical skills. This book consists of a vast variety of questions, including multiple choice questions, and long and short answer-type questions. It follows the lower and higher order of Bloom's taxonomy. The lower order leads the students to understand, remember and apply for practical applications. Higher order skills improve students' creativity, analysis, and evaluation skills. It also contains experiments at the end of the chapter which will help students to apply the content on practical applications. Each chapter has references and recommended readings through which students can explore more theoretical and practical aspects of the main content. Beside these, it also consists of 'Know More' section to discuss the additional information about the content.

The author sincerely hopes that the book will motivate the students to learn and apply the MATLAB programming to practical applications and will surely contribute to the research and development in the engineering field. The author welcomes all beneficial comments and suggestions to improve the future editions of the book. It gives an immense pleasure to place this book in the hands of the teachers and students.

Hari Prabhat Gupta
Indian Institute of Technology (BHU) Varanasi, India

OUTCOME BASED EDUCATION

For the implementation of an outcome based education the first requirement is to develop an outcome based curriculum and incorporate an outcome based assessment in the education system. By going through outcome based assessments evaluators will be able to evaluate whether the students have achieved the outlined standard, specific and measurable outcomes. With the proper incorporation of outcome based education there will be a definite commitment to achieve a minimum standard for all learners without giving up at any level. At the end of the programme running with the aid of outcome based education, a students will be able to arrive at the following outcomes:

PO-1 Engineering knowledge

PO-2 Problem analysis

PO-3 Design/development of solutions

PO-4 Conduct investigations of complex problems

PO-5 Modern tool usage

PO-6 The engineer and society

PO-7 Environment and sustainability

PO-8 Ethics

PO-9 Individual and team work

PO-10 Communication

PO-11 Project management and finance

PO-12 Life-long learning

COURSE OUTCOMES

After course completion, the students will be able to:

CO-1: Understand the fundamentals of MATLAB and Creating MATLAB variables,workspace and miscellaneous commands.

CO-2: Practice the matrix, array and basic mathematical functions, solving linearequations, and other mathematical functions.

CO-3: Analyze the programming script with input/output, script side-effects and anatomyof a M-File function.

CO-4: Develop script with relational and logical operators, "for…end" loop, "while….end" loop, other flow structures, operator precedence, saving output to a file

CO-5: Understand the Debugging process, running with breakpoints, examining values, correcting and ending debugging and correcting an M-file.

Course Outcome	**Expected Mapping with Programme Outcomes** (1-Weak Correlation; 2-Medium correlation; 3-Strong Correlation)											
	PO-1	**PO-2**	**PO-3**	**PO-4**	**PO-5**	**PO-6**	**PO-7**	**PO-8**	**PO-9**	**PO-10**	**PO-11**	**PO-12**
CO-1	3	3	3	1	-	-	-	-	1	1	1	3
CO-2	1	2	3	3	3	3	3	3	2	1	3	3
CO-3	1	2	3	3	3	3	3	3	2	1	3	3
CO-4	1	2	3	3	3	3	3	3	2	1	3	3
CO-5	2	2	3	3	3	3	3	3	2	2	1	2

GUIDELINES FOR TEACHERS

Outcome Based Education (OBE) aims at improving student's skills and knowledge. Therefore, it becomes the teacher's responsibility to implement OBE in an appropriate and systematic way. Following are some responsibilities (not limited to) are given below:

- The teachers must provide the exercise so that students can explore more and more.
- The students must have an online or offline version of the MATLAB without considering any other potential ineligibility.
- The teachers must try to enhance the students skills and logical skills while pursuing the course.
- Every student must be accoutred with quality of education appended with competence after they finalized their education.
- They must always motivate the students to enhance their quintessential performanceby their capabilities.
- The teachers must promote and motivate the team work as it creates the interest andcuriosity amongst the students.
- They must ensure Bloom's taxonomy as shown in Figure I during the assessment and evaluation of the students. The detailed explanation of Bloom's Taxonomy is given in Table I.

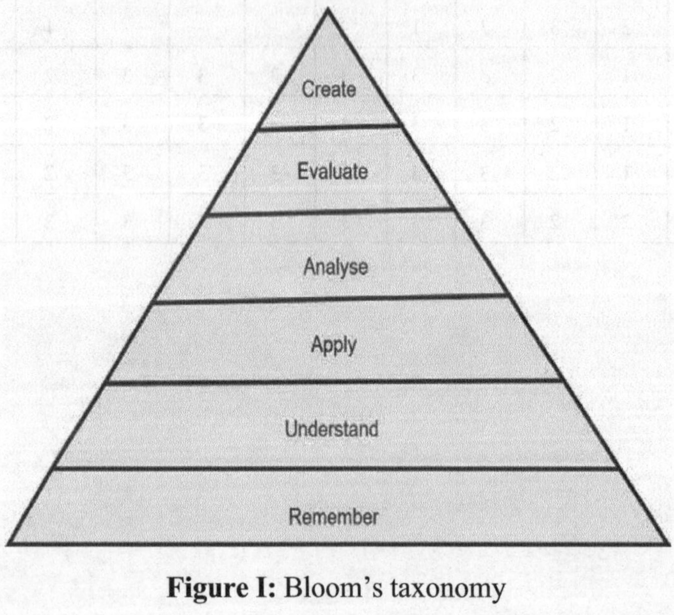

Figure I: Bloom's taxonomy

Table I: Bloom's Taxonomy

Level	Teacher should check thestudent's ability to	Student should beable to	Possible Mode of Assessment
Create	create	design or fabricateor simulate	Mini or majorproject
Evaluate	justify	secure or defend	Assignment
Analyse	distinguish	characterize ordistinguish	Project/lab methodology
Apply	use information	operate orillustrate	Technical presentation/ illustration
Understand	explain the ideas	explain or describe	Presentation/seminar
Remember	define (or remember)	define or remember	Quiz

GUIDELINES FOR STUDENTS

Students must opt for equal responsibility for simulating the OBE. Following are someresponsibilities (not limited to):

- Students must be familiar with each unit outcome before starting the new unit.
- Students must be familiar with each course outcome before starting the course.
- Students must be familiar with each programme outcome before starting theprogramme.
- Students must properly apply the concept to practical problems.
- Student's learning must be related to practical and real life consequences.
- Students must be familiar with their competency at every level of OBE.

LIST OF ABBREVIATIONS			
Abbreviation	**Full form**	**Abbreviation**	**Full form**
2D	2-Dimensional	IT	Information Technology
3D	3-Dimensional	IoT	Internet of things
FPGA	Field Programmable GateArrays	PLC	Programmable LogicController
GPU	Graphics Processing Unit	MATLAB	MATrix LABoratory
HDL	Hardware Description Language	RAM	Random AccessMemory
HTML	HyperText Markup Language	SCILAB	Scientific Laboratory

LIST OF FIGURES

LIST OF TABLES

LIST OF EXPERIMENTS		
1	Experiment 4.1: Experiment on vector operation	94
2	Experiment 4.2: Experiment on matrix operation	96
3	Experiment 4.3: Generation of signal waveform	98
4	Experiment 4.4: MATLAB program on convolution process	99
5	Experiment 6.1: Experiment on conditional branching	148
6	Experiment 8.1: Extract features of an image using MATLAB	181
7	Experiment 8.2: MATLAB program for image negation	182
8	Experiment 8.3: MATLAB program for power law transformation	184
9	Experiment 8.4: File handling in MATLAB	185

Contents

1 Introduction to IT Workshop

UNIT SPECIFICS

This unit covers the following aspects:

- *About IT Workshop*
- *IT Workshop using MATLAB, Python, scripting language*
- *Applications of IT Workshop*
- *IT Workshop for research and development*
- *Organization of the book*

This unit familiarizes the students with the Information Technology (IT) Workshop. It discusses the different platforms and applications of IT Workshop. This unit also discusses the various challenges in the IT field, which helps the students to explore new ideas. The research and development aspects of IT Workshop are also covered to develop the student's curiosity about developing new technologies. Finally, it discusses the structure of the book. At the end of the Unit, it consists of several references and recommended readings that help students explore more theoretical and practical aspects of the main content.

RATIONALE

This unit initially introduces the IT Workshop. It then discusses the IT Workshop using MATLAB, Python, and scripting languages. It discusses the various applications of IT Workshop in different domains, e.g., biomedical engineering, wireless communication, signal processing, image processing, control, financial systems, etc. Next, it discusses the challenges in the information technology field, which include IT domain liability, data security, open source software, etc. This unit also covers the IT Workshop for research and development.

PRE-REQUISITES

Basic knowledge of information technology

UNIT OUTCOMES

The outcomes of the Unit are as follows:

U1-O1: Describe IT Workshop

U1-O2: Discuss the IT Workshop using MATLAB, Python, and scripting language

U1-O3: Discuss the applications and challenges of information technology

U1-O4: IT Workshop for research and development

Unit-1 Outcomes	EXPECTED MAPPING WITH COURSE OUTCOMES (1- Weak Correlation; 2- Medium correlation; 3- Strong Correlation)				
	CO-1	CO-2	CO-3	CO-4	CO-5
U1-O1	3	-	1	-	-
U1-O2	2	-	1	-	1
U1-O3	3	-	-	-	-
U1-O4	3	-	-	-	-

1.1 About IT Workshop

Information Technology (IT) Workshop includes the implementation, advancement, and reinforcement of computer-based information technologies. In the last few decades, IT has been impelled by scientists and academicians. This era of IT has merged a global network that is used to transmit information using modern technologies. It has a wide range of applications in communication systems, intelligent transportation systems, digital circuits, etc. For practical implementation of these applications, it requires a platform that consists of algorithms and mechanisms in terms of mathematical formulation. The platform includes programming languages.

1.2 IT Workshop in different domains

The different programming languages, e.g., MATLAB, Python, scripting language, etc., can be used to solve different scientific problems. These consist of various toolboxes to model the complex expressions to simple manipulations. Based on the methodology and available toolboxes, the user opts for the domains to perform the arithmetic, relational, and logical operations. IT Workshop can be done in MATLAB, Python, scripting language, and other computer programming languages. The rest of this section discusses the programming of IT Workshop in MATLAB, Python, and scripting languages.

1.2.1 IT Workshop using MATLAB

MATLAB is the most widely used programming language to simulate mathematical expressions [1]. It gives the output in terms of numeric values, arrays, or graphical representation. It is the ideal choice for moderate and complex mathematical manipulation. It consists of many toolboxes with applications in engineering science, biological science, financial management, etc. The most commonly used toolboxes include signal processing, control, image, communication, etc. The users can operate MATLAB online and offline, making this more user-friendly.

SCAN ME
for more about MATLAB

1.2.2 IT Workshop using Python

Guido van Rossum developed the Python programming language in the late 1980s. The initial version was made accessible in 1991 and gained huge popularity amongst the researchers and academicians. For this contribution, Guido van Rossum was entitled as 'Benevolent Dictator for Life' by the Python group. Python is a high-level and multi-paradigm computer programming language licensed under a General Public License (GPL) [2]. It is an open-source platform authorized by OSI and FSF. It consists the applications in web-based systems, mathematical computation, machine learning, deep learning algorithms, etc. Due to its compact syntax, it allows users to write simple program statements for complex expressions. It contains innumerable inbuilt libraries and functions to perform the task. The significant

SCAN ME
for more about Python

advantage of Python is that it is easy to understand, apply to real-world problems, and inbuilt functions and libraries.

Key features: *Python is one of the popular programming languages nowadays due to its magnificent performance. Following are the key features of Python which makes it highly demanding platform for professionals:*

- **Easy to apply:** *Python is easy to learn and apply for practical application. It consists of ingenious syntax which can be easily learnt and applied by the beginners.*
- **Compact syntax:** *Python uses the compact syntax which helps the users to write the short program for the complex expressions. This makes this programming language more user friendly.*
- **Freely available:** *Python is licensed under the GPL. This makes this programming language as freely accessible. It can be download from the Python's official site i.e., Python Releases for Windows | Python.org.*
- **Interactive and dynamic programming:** *It uses chevron prompt (>>>) which allows the user to write and simulate the program statement spontaneously. This feature becomes useful when a program statement has errors and it requires debugging techniques. Python is also a dynamic programming as users need not to define the datatype as they are already defined.*
- **Portability and scalability:** *Python is compatible with operating systems e.g. Windows, Linux, MacOS. These support a favourable executing environment for writing the complex expressions.*
- **Huge library:** *Python has a huge inbuilt library and function which makes this programming language as user friendly.*
- **Memory management:** *Python consists of a garbage collector for memory management. Thus, memory allocation is not an issue for users.*

1.2.3 IT Workshop using scripting language

The HyperText Markup Language, abbreviated as HTML, is a scripting language [3] to design the documents. HTML was introduced by physicist Tim Berners-Lee in the early 1990s. It was then made available for users in late 1991 in the form of a document named 'HTML Tags'. Since then, it has been updated many times since it was first released. Its latest version is HTML 5. Table 1.1 describes the different versions of HTML. These documents can be presented in a web browser. It is widely used for developing web pages and enhancing data storage. It has applications in internet navigation. Due to webpage support, easier to learn, and faster to code, scripting languages such as HTML are preferable for IT Workshop. It is now developed and maintained by Web Hypertext Application Technology Working Group (WHATWG).

SCAN ME
for more about HTML

Table 1.1: *Different versions of HTML.*

Versions	Released on	Descriptions
HTML1	1991	• *Initial Version* • *Consists of 18 elements* • *Tim Berners-Lee contemplate HTML as elevance of SGNL*
HTML2	1995	• *New feature added* • *Maintained by W3C*
HTML3	1997	• *Released with novel features i.e., tables, scripts, etc.* • *Text with images also improved*
HTML4	1997	• *New features i.e., style sheets, added* • *Introduced CSS*
HTML5	2014	• *It is a latest version* • *It comes with advanced features e.g., videos insertion, improved content layout, etc.*

Features of HTML:

- **Easy to operate:** *HTML is a simple and straightforward language that is easy to apply for practical usage.*
- **Platform-independent:** *Major advantage of HTML is that it is platform independent scripting language unlike other languages like Java, C/C++ etc.*
- **Webpage development:** *This language allows images and audio inclusion on the webpage. Latest version of HTML allows the video insertion to the webpage.*
- **Hypertext inclusion:** *It also allows the hypertext included to the text which can be displayed on electronic devices. The users can spontaneously access the link which is referenced to the hypertext.*
- **Markup language:** *The users can supervise the exhibit of the document.*

Demerits of HTML: *Apart from the merits, HTML scripting language has disadvantages also. Some of major disadvantages are given below:*

- *This language allows us to generate static web pages. It fails to generate dynamic web pages.*
- *This language does not have compact syntax. Thus, it uses complex programs for generating a simple webpage.*
- *It does not allow mathematical computation or mathematical simulation.*

IT Workshop can be accomplished using different platforms. The scripting languages, such as HTML, are specially developed for web development. It is challenging to use such scripting languages for mathematical computation. Python consists of several libraries that are freely available for users. However, this platform is limited by the availability of different domain toolboxes. MATLAB consists of many toolboxes for various applications in engineering science, biomedical science, financial management, etc. MATLAB is available in online as well as offline modes. Moreover, MATLAB consists of the tools for almost all engineering branches. Such benefits and unique features of MATLAB, makes it suitable for IT Workshop. This book uses MATLAB for the programming of IT Workshop.

1.3 Applications of IT Workshop

IT Workshop has numerous applications in engineering, management, and medical sciences. In this section, we discuss some applications of IT Workshop. We also discuss the available packages in MATLAB for the applications.

- **Wireless communication systems:** *The signal of different frequencies can be transmitted from one place to another using wireless communication. The devices at the transmitter and receiver can be synchronized using MATLAB programming. They have applications in 5G, satellite communication, long-term evolution systems, designing of radio frequency antennas, etc.*
- **Control systems:** *The control systems stabilize the devices using the looping systems. MATLAB contains a control system toolbox to operate these systems. The algorithms in the toolbox can analyze the system performance in both time and frequency domains. It consists of several controllers for tuning the gain of the systems.*
- **Image processing:** *The low-quality image can be enhanced using image processing techniques. The image processing can be analog or digital. Digital image processing is more popular among these two. MATLAB consists of a separate image processing toolbox to process the images.*
- **Internet of Things:** *The Internet of Things (IoT) connects devices with the outside world using the internet. Examples of IoT analytics platform services are ThingSpeak and Amazon Web Services (AWS). Such platforms lead to storing and analyzing data through cloud computing. The users can also compare the data with the historical data available for better output by removing noise, disturbances, outliers, etc.*
- **Signal processing:** *MATLAB can also be used to analyze, supervise and control the time-variant and time-invariant signal. It has a signal processing toolbox for this purpose which consists of numerous algorithms for signal operations, e.g., quantization, upsampling, downsampling, filtering, etc. It can operate in both*

domains, i.e., the time and frequency domains. It also helps to develop wave signal datasets, which can be further processed using artificial intelligence model training.

- **Embedded systems:** *Embedded systems are the combination of software and hardware that are designed to perform a specific task. Such systems have a wide range of real-time applications, including smartphones, UAVs, and transportation systems. The practicability of these systems becomes easy when designed and simulated using MATLAB and Simulink.*
- **Mechatronics:** *Mechatronics is the amalgamation of mechanics and electronics. Thus, the integration of physical systems and embedded systems perform the tasks. It initially recognizes the simulated algorithms and then operates in parallel to obtain the optimum results. As it performs operations with hardware, thus causing an error in the output. The algorithms for the system models are designed to overcome these issues.*
- **Computational biology:** *In this methodology, scientists analyze the biological conduct using mathematical formulation and simulation. MATLAB allows these mathematical expressions to simulate and predict the behavior. The users can model the algorithms for generating innovative formulations.*
- **Computational finance:** *It deals with risk & investment regulation, insurance, etc. MATLAB allows the user to analyze live market data and helps in mathematical modeling. It also estimates the risk attributions and provides the solution for minimum risk.*
- **Motor and power control:** *It modulates the motor torque, speed, and other parameters to ensure stability. MATLAB provides cost-effective design, which leads to productive processors, sensors, etc. It also allows Hardware Description Language (HDL) for testing and simulation.*
- **Robotics:** *Robotics helps in designing and implementing autonomous systems. MATLAB contains algorithms that can read and analyze the data from the robotics system, which can be implemented for hardware-in-the-loop tests for further verification.*
- **FPGA Design and Codesign:** *Field Programmable Gate Arrays (FPGA) consist of configurable logic blocks programmed according to user needs. The programmable behavior of FPGA makes it worthy for several applications, including wireless sensor networks, communication systems, biomedical devices, etc. MATLAB allows innovation of the prototype and system on chip devices. It helps the users to implement and debug the FPGA program and develop model hardware architectonic.*

1.4 Challenges

IT has become very popular in the last few decades due to its manifold-cloud domain. The researchers are adopting new technologies to develop the infrastructure models. These lead to easy sharing of information. However, this easy availability of huge data and exploration of businesses result in expanding privacy and security risks. The following are the major challenges in IT:

1. **IT domain liabilities:** *Digital transformation needs advanced emerging technologies and new frameworks. It becomes necessary to endorse the appropriate and skilled leader. Therefore it is necessary to escalate the skilled leader. Appended to this, skilled workers in this field must also be embellished.*
2. **Information security:** *Technological advancement leads to information security concerns. The information security concern pervades almost all new technologies, including professional and personal data saved on the cloud.*
3. **Effective mathematical computation:** *The real application in IT involves a huge amount of data continuously varying with time. Most of these require a high-end processing unit for further analyzing and processing.*
4. **Open source platform:** *Although the open source platforms lead to ease of manipulation but these compromise ownership of organization products. These are not safe for confidential business transactions.*
5. **Remote automation:** *New technology advancements are resulting in smart homes, offices, and cities that can be grandiose by several accidents and disturbances. This needs a breach of regulations between the customer and the service provider.*

1.5 IT Workshop for research and development

The main aim of the IT Workshop is to foster research and development in engineering science, medical science, etc. Different IT domains have abundant research fields, including global positioning satellites, digital circuit design, remote areas communication, medical appliances, etc. MATLAB enables researchers to design and simulate model-based systems to analyze and develop the most efficient system. Platforms such as MATLAB, Simulink, Python, etc. allow researchers first to delineate the system model and then test on these platforms before practical implementation. This helps to develop a cost-efficient and accurate model for a system.

1.6 Organization of the book

The remainder of the book is structured as follows: Chapter 2 introduces MATLAB and its tools. It also discusses the installation methods appended with the applications of MATLAB. Chapter 3 discusses the variables with their naming convention. It also includes operators, i.e., arithmetic, logical, relational operators, and rational expressions. Chapter 4 covers the vectors, matrices, and various operations such as arithmetic, relational, and logic with vectors and matrices. Chapter 5 introduces MATLAB scripts and functions. It also consists of various types of functions with applications. Chapter 6 contains branch statements, i.e., if, if-else, nested if-else, switch-case statements, etc. Besides these, it also covers 'is' function and its application. Chapter 7 includes loop statements, e.g., for loop, nested for loop, while loop, etc. It also introduces the time function and its application in signal processing. Chapter 8 discusses the basics of image processing, i.e., importing, exporting and performing image transformation. It covers histogram equalization, linear transformation, logarithmic transformation, and power law transformation methods. This unit also includes file handling in MATLAB. Finally, Chapter 9 introduces MATLAB program organization. It then discusses the menu-driven modular program and debugging techniques that help remove errors in the program statements. It also introduces SCILAB programming.

Unit Summary

- *The programming languages, e.g., MATLAB, Python, HTML, etc., are used to solve several problems in the field of engineering, management, and medical sciences.*
  - *MATLAB is a high-level programming language that can be used for numeric calculation, advanced graphics, and visualization.*
  - *Python is a high-level and multi-paradigm computer programming language licensed under a general public license.*
  - *HTML is a markup language that is mainly used for designing documents.*
- *IT Workshop consists various applications,such as*
  - *Wireless communication and control systems*
  - *Image and signal processing*
  - *Internet of things*
  - *Mechatronics and robotics*
  - *Computational biology and finance*
  - *Motor and power control*
  - *FPGA Design and Codesign*
- *Major challenges in IT fields are*
  - *IT domain liabilities*
  - *Information security*
  - *Effective mathematical computation*
  - *Open source platform*
  - *Remote automation*

Short and Long Answer Type Questions

1.1 *Explain the significance of IT Workshop in brief.*

1.2 *Write a short note on the following*
  - *(a) IT Workshop using MATLAB*
  - *(b) IT Workshop using Python*
  - *(c) IT Workshop using HTML*

1.3 *What are the applications of IT Workshop?*

1.4 *What are the major challenges of information technology? Explain in brief.*

1.5 *Explain the significance of IT Workshops in research and development.*

1.6 *What are the key features of the Python language?*

1.7 *What are the key features of HTML scripting language?*

References

[1] *'Applications of MATLAB', 2022 [Online]. Available: https://www.mathworks.com/help/simulink/applications.html [Accessed: September-2022].*

[2] *'Introduction of Python, 2022 [Online]. Available: https://www.python.org/ [Accessed: September-2022].*

[3] *'Introduction of HTML', 2022 [Online]. Available: https://html.spec.whatwg.org/multipage/ [Accessed: September-2022].*

2 Introduction to MATLAB

UNIT SPECIFICS

Through this unit we have discussed the following aspects:

- *About MATLAB and its tools*
- *Installation of MATLAB using online and offline*
- *Use of MATLAB in different domains*

This unit discusses the preliminaries of MATLAB for developing further curiosity and inventiveness. This also explains the different modes of operation of MATLAB, which will help students to apply in practical applications, not only in engineering science but also in finance, biological science, etc.

At the end of the main contents of the unit, a variety of questions are given. These follow the lower and higher order of Bloom's taxonomy. These questions let the students gain more insight into the content and improve their logical skills. It also enlisted references and recommended readings which helps the students to explore more about the content.

There is one more section named "Know More". This section discusses the inventor of MATLAB. To create interest among students, this section highlights the developing phase of MATLAB and its developer, i.e., MathWorks.

RATIONALE

This preliminary unit helps students to get a basic idea about MATLAB. It describes the history of the development of MATLAB and MathWorks organization. This unit also helps students to explore the different toolboxes available in MATLAB and Simulink. The MATLAB environment is also discussed, including the command window, editor window, and workspace window. This unit elucidates the basic idea of introducing input using the command window and editor window. It exclusively explains the installation of MATLAB products using both, with and without an internet connection. MATLAB online is also gaining popularity nowadays. This unit gives further distinct ideas of MATLAB online mode. Several toolboxes, along with their applications, are also discussed in this unit. Simultaneously, it considers the merits and demerits of the online and offline modes of MATLAB usage. A brief cloud solution is also discussed in this unit.

PRE-REQUISITES

Basic use of computers

Basic knowledge of computer programming

UNIT OUTCOMES

List of outcomes of this unit is as follows:

U2-O1: About MATLAB

U2-O2: Installation of MATLAB

U2-O3: Use of MATLAB

Unit-2 Outcomes	EXPECTED MAPPING WITH COURSE OUTCOMES (1- Weak Correlation; 2- Medium correlation; 3- Strong Correlation)				
	CO-1	CO-2	CO-3	CO-4	CO-5
U2-O1	3	-	-	-	1
U2-O2	3	-	-	-	1
U2-O3	3	1	1	1	1

2.1 About MATLAB

MATLAB is an integrated technical computing environment that amalgamates numeric calculation, advanced graphics and visualization, and a high-level programming language [1]. MATLAB is derived from the word MATrix LABoratory. It is a widely-used programming language for mathematical computation and graphical representation. MATLAB was designed by Cleve Moler in the late 1960s, and it first appeared in the late 1970s for simple matrix calculations. MATLAB was commercially released by MathWorks, Inc. in 1984. In the 1990s, MathWorks introduced the first MATLAB compiler. Later, MathWorks added important libraries and toolboxes that support Graphics Processing Units (GPUs). Recently, MathWorks launched many features, e.g., MATLAB live editor notebook, to improve the interfacing and functionality. The latest version of MATLAB is R2022a released in March 2022.

Besides MATLAB, Simulink is also the primary product of MathWorks. Simulink is a MATLAB-based graphical programming platform. Simulink has a wide range of applicationsin control systems and signal processing for system design and simulation. Simulink is especially useful in one's growth process. It helps the users to get novel ideas, and then,they can create the code for the system and check for the results. The user can do the multiple executions of the program and recreates the code for optimal results [2].

Several categories of MATLAB inbuilt examples are available, which can be used by students and working professionals. MATLAB and Simulink are basically potent mathematical tools that consist of several varieties of toolboxes. The important MATLAB applications and the toolbox are as follows [3]:

SCAN ME
For more about MATLAB applications

- **Signal processing:** *The toolbox available in MATLAB for this application are audio, SerDes toolbox RF, DSP, phased array systems, sensor fusion, tracking, signal processing, and wavelet toolbox.*
- **Control system:** *Aerospace, automated driving, control system, fuzzy logic, model predictive and robotics toolbox, system identification are the toolbox of control system application.*
- **Wireless communication:** *5G Antenna, LTE HDL, wireless local area network toolbox.*
- **Code generation:** *Embedded, filter designing, HDL, GPU, MATLAB coder, filter design HDL coder, Fixed-point designer, Vision HDL toolbox.*
- **Math, statistics, and optimization:** *Curve fitting, mapping, global optimization, Model-based calibration, Partial differential equation, Symbolic math, and optimization.*
- **Data science, machine and deep learning:** *Deep & machine learning statistics, Predictive maintenance, Reinforcement learning, Text analytics.*
- **Image processing and segmentation, computer vision:** *Automated driving system, Computer vision, Image acquisition, Vision hardware description language.*
- **Financial management system:** *Database toolbox, Datafeed econometrics, Finance instruments, Finance and risk management, Spreadsheet link, trading.*
- **Computational biological system:** *Bioinformatics, SimBiology.*

- **Application deployment:** *MATLAB compiler, MATLAB compiler software, development kit.*

The toolbox available for important applications of Simulink are as follows [3]:

- **Signal processing:** *Audio & SerDes toolbox, RF, digital signal processing system, Mixed-signal blockset, Phased array system.*
- **Control system:** *Aerospace and powertrain, Vehicle dynamics blockset, Robotics system and control design, Design optimization.*
- **Wireless communication:** *Communication toolbox.*
- **Code generation:** *AUTOSAR blockset, Kit for DO qualification, Embedded, Simulink, HDL, PLC coder, Fixed-Point designer, IEC certification kit, LTE HDL toolbox, Simulink code inspector.*

MATLAB provides a rich user experience design. The shortcut icon of the MATLAB is shown as . Figure 2.1 illustrates a default layout of MATLAB. The three different types of windows, namely Command Window, Editor Window, and Workspace appear on the default layout of MATLAB.

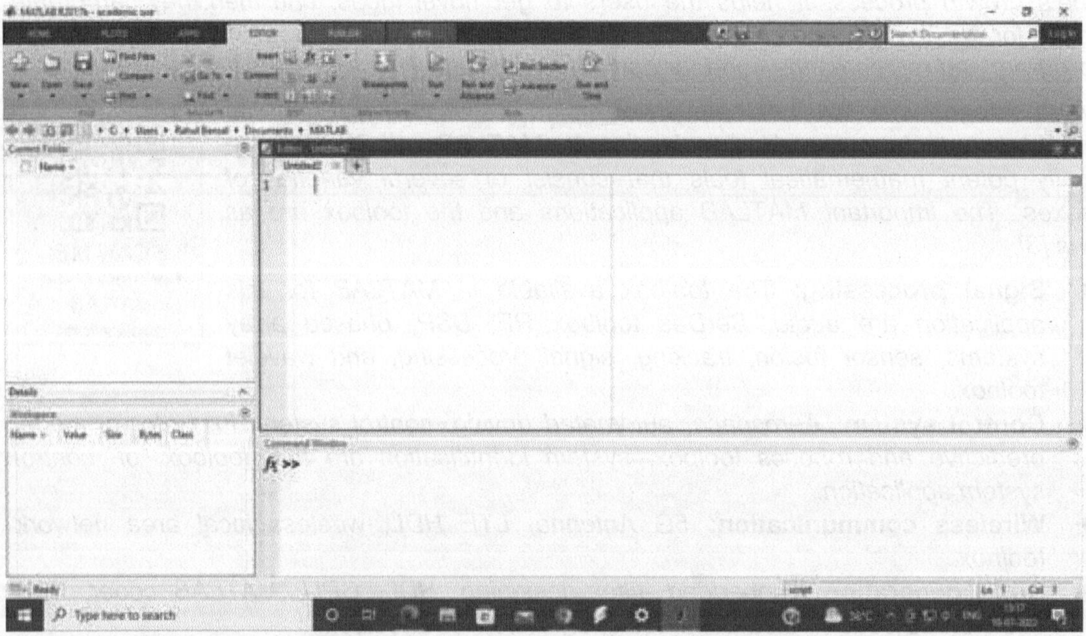

Figure 2.1: *Illustration of MATLAB default layout.*

The **command window** *is the most crucial part of all the windows. The symbol ">>", also known as prompt, is used to execute a MATLAB command and gives the corresponding outcome instantly. It is quite interesting to know that the command window uses its inbuilt workspace which can be displayed in the workspace window.*

MATLAB has the Help section which can be operated either directly from the starting window as shown in Figure 2.1 or by typing help appended with command or function name in the command window. The command window can be cleared using the clc command at the prompt.

The **editor window** *consists of commands (program) that are saved in MATLAB files. It can be seen on the upper portion of the command window as shown in Figure 2.1. The commands can be edited in the editor window (which are permanently saved in MATLAB file) and corresponding outcomes can be seen in the command window and workspace.*

The **workspace window** *comprises numeric values of the variables in the form of outcome. It also consists of data that is imported into MATLAB. The utilization of the workspace window becomes crucial for a long MATLAB program that consists of many variables. The workspace window enlists all the variables and their corresponding values. It also displays the size, memory allocated, class associated with the variables. Figure 2.2 illustrates the workspace window.*

Workspace

Name	Value	Size	Bytes	Class	Range
Delhi_Humidity	48	1x1	8	double	0
Delhi_Temp	40	1x1	8	double	0
Height	5.5000	1x1	8	double	0
Jammu_Humidity	55	1x1	8	double	0
Jammu_Temp	-1	1x1	8	double	0
Weight	80	1x1	8	double	0

Figure 2.2: *Workspace layout in MATLAB.*

The workspace becomes empty whenever the user exits the program without saving. The data will reappear in the workspace after the execution of the program. Saving the long and complex MATLAB program periodically will help avoid rewriting the program.

Command history in MATLAB can be seen at the bottom of the workspace window. It uses to show the already executed commands in the past. The reuse of the long and complex commands using from command history reduces the time of the user. A command namely, whos, in MATLAB enlists the variables appended with their size in a MATLAB program. When the user clicks on a particular variable, it will display the values assigned to the variable in a new tab referred to as array editor.

We can give the input in MATLAB in two ways: the command window and the editor window. These inputs can be in the form of variables or numeric values. Working in the command window is helpful for the short program statement due to its command history characteristics. The major advantage of introducing input to the command window is to show the corresponding output value spontaneously. It also requires memory space when the program is being executed. However, such practice doesn't save the program and the workspace becomes empty whenever the user exits. Variable values or data are neither saved in the command window nor in the workspace window when the program will close. The editor window overcomes the above limitations. To use the editor window, create a m-file by clicking on Create new document→Script menu as shown in Figure 2.1 and save the file at the desired location using the Save document icon. A major advantage of using the editor window is that the program statements are saved in memory as m-file format. MATLAB displays the output in the command window in the form of numerical or text values. MATLAB consists of a window, known as a graphical window, to display the outputs in graph format. The graphical window can be further edited as the user requirements.

2.2 Installation of MATLAB

MathWorks allows the installation of MATLAB using standard installation and installation without using internet connection methods. Before installing the latest version of MATLAB i.e., R2022a on a system, the user must ensure several requirements which need to be fulfilled. The system requirements for installing MATLAB R2022a are as follows [4]:

SCAN ME
For more about system requirements

- **Operating system:** *MATLAB supports Windows (Version 10, version 11, and Server 2019 of Windows) and Mac (Monterey (version 12), Big Sur (version 11.6), and Catalina (version 10.15.7) of macOS) operating system. It also supports Linux operating systems with Ubuntu version 20.04 LTS and version 18.04 LTS, Debian 10, Red Hat Enterprise Linux version 8 and version 7, SUSE Linux Enterprise Desktop version 12 and version 15, and SUSE Linux Enterprise Server version 1 and 12.*
- **Processor:** *MATLAB is compatible with all Intel processors and AMD x86-64 when operated with Windows, Mac and Linux. Besides the aforementioned processor, MATLAB also supports (Apple silicon) in Mac.*
- **RAM:** *It requires a minimum 4GB RAM to work with MATLAB. However, it is recommended to use 8GB RAM for better performance.*
- **Storage:** *It needs around 3.5 GB for MATLAB, 5GB to 8GB for typical installation. Complete installation requires 24GB for Mac & Linux and 31.5GB for Windows. Users are recommended to use SSD for better performance while working with MATLAB.*
- **Graphics:** *There is no need for specific graphics cards for running Windows, Mac, and Linux operating systems. However, MathWorks recommends 1GB GPU for better performance.*

The following points should be noted while installing MATLAB:

- *Windows 7 is not supported in the MATLAB latest version R2022a.*
- *MATLAB also supports operation on shared computers. Shared computer installation requires permission from the administrator.*
- *Many times, it requires altering the tmp folder. The procedure can be followed from the link [5].*

The following two ways are possible to install MATLAB:

I. **Standard installation:** *In the standard installation method, MATLAB is installed on a computer using an internet connection. The user first needs to create a MathWorks* *account. It is advised to disable the antivirus during installation as it leads to slow down the installation process due to insignificant internet security applications. Before the installation process starts, some system requirements for the latest version need to be fulfilled, as discussed above. The following steps are involved in installing MATLAB using standard installation [6]:*

Step 1. *Create a MathWorks account and sign up. If MathWorks account is not available personally, you can sign up using the university's or company's license.*

Step 2. *Download the release from the official website of MATLAB and run the installer. You must agree to make the changes when it will suggest.*

Step 3. *The next step is a license agreement between the user and MathWorks. It is mandatory to accept the agreement otherwise it is not possible to install the MATLAB.*

Step 4. *It will ask for the activation key and authentication.*

Step 5. *After authentication, you can select the destination folder then MATLAB product needs to be selected.*

Step 6. *The last step is confirmation from the user and installation is done. After installation, click Finish to complete the installation.*

II. **Without using internet connection:** *In this method, the installation is accomplished using a file installation key. Initially, the user must obtain the license center's installation key. The following steps are performed for installation [7]:*

Step 1. *Sign up to the MathWorks account on a computer with an internet connection and download the MATLAB product on removable storage memory along with the license.*

Step 2. *Next, the license file and installation key need to be copied to the target computer.*

Step 3. *After obtaining the installer and MATLAB product files, the next step is to start the installer. It will also take permission for the app to make changes, which is to be accepted for further processing.*

Step 4. *MathWorks asks to agree to all the terms and conditions related to the software license agreement. The MATLAB products will not be installed if the user does not accept these agreements.*

Step 5. *Next, the user needs to enter the installation key.*

Note: *If a user has the incorrect installation key, then the user may ask for a new one.*

Step 6. *Offline MATLAB installation needs a license file to install the MATLAB product. If the user selects a license file for a different MATLAB product, it will show an error. Therefore, the selection of the correct license file for the correct MATLAB product is compulsory. The user can ask for a new license file if the installer identifies any incorrect license file.*

Step 7. *MathWorks products can be installed in the default destination folder or the user's choice folder (recommended by MathWorks). If the destination folder is the user's choice, the following are the specifications while selecting the folder name:*

- *Non-English characters are not allowed.*
- *Alphanumeric characters and special characters e.g., underscore, are valid.*
- *Function names can not be folder names.*

Step 8. *The user can select the product associated with the installation key. There are several MATLAB products that are dependent on each other, the user will get a product dependency warning while selecting such products.*

Step 9. *The user selects an option to create a shortcut icon, symbolic links, or mex script based on the operating system.*

Step 10. *The next step is to review the product summary and click on begin the installation.*

Step 11. *After completion of the installation, the user can click on finish to complete the installation.*

Note:

- *MathWorks allows the installation of the products non-interactively. If a user needs to install several MATLAB products with the same information, then the user can use the information through the properties file. This time-saving process is very useful for reducing installation errors.*
- *MATLAB communicates with MathWorks to check the license validity from time to time. It also allows the user to update the license if its time period is over.*
- *Mathworks allows installing its product for multiple computers. For this, the user must contact the administrator.*

2.3 Use of MATLAB

Similar to the installation of MATLAB, it can be accessed in online and offline modes.

2.3.1 MATLAB online

MATLAB online was released in March 2017. It enables the user to access MATLAB products using any standard web browser with an internet connection. This feature leads to a revolutionary leap by providing an online platform for the users to access MATLAB. It has become very useful, especially for working professionals, MATLAB training for researchers and young minds to explore the MATLAB products. After releasing in 2017, MATLAB online is expanding day by day to the demand of the users. Table 2.1 shows the supported products in MATLAB online.

SCAN ME
For more about online supported products

Table 2.1: *MATLAB online supported products [8].*

Products	**Applications**
Toolbox for 5G	*5G toolbox has applications in RF designs, interference sources, and 5G new radio communication systems.*
Aerospace toolbox	*This toolbox has applications in aerospace engineering, 2-dimensional and 3-dimensional visualization of vehicle movement, analyzing satellite motion.*
Audio toolbox	*Audio toolbox helps in acoustic signal modeling which can analyze audio features. The results are further trained using computer programming.*
Computer vision toolbox	*This toolbox has applications in 3-dimensional vision, and video processing frameworks. This is also compatible with other programming language like C/C++.*
DSP system toolbox	*DSP system toolbox has several applications e.g., signal processing systems, RF systems, RADAR, telecommunication, finite and infinite system response systems, etc. It also supports C/C++ code for system modeling.*
Image processing toolbox	*Using this toolbox, any image can be enhanced, segmented, or further processed to remove noise or further processing.*
Database toolbox	*It helps in interchanging the data from different databases.*
LTE toolbox	*This toolbox gives long-term evolution (LTE) modeling and designing for communication systems. It is also compatible with radio frequency hardware.*
GPU coder	*It is used for CUDA kernels code creation for deep learning, DSP systems, etc.*
MATLAB coder	*This toolbox helps in creating programming codes for MATLAB which are compatible with the hardware.*
Model predictive control toolbox	*It helps in modeling and simulation of the different controllers.*
Parallel computing toolbox	*This toolbox has different processors, GPUs, and several clusters which helps in resolving data-intensive issues.*

Robotics system toolbox	*It helps in modeling and simulation of mobile robots, industrial robots, etc.*
Satellite communications	*Satellite communications toolbox has applications in modeling and testing satellite communication systems.*
Signal processing toolbox	*This toolbox helps to model various signal processing filters, which leads to resampling, smoothing, and further analyzing the signal. It also supports an artificial intelligence model for signal improvement.*
Simscape multibody	*Simscape helps in modeling of physical systems e.g., rectifiers, electric motors etc.*
Simulink coder	*This toolbox creates C/C++ codes for MATLAB. For this reason, it was called a real-time workshop.*
Simulink control design	*It helps in designing and modeling control systems e.g., PID controllers.*
Simulink design optimization	*It gives tools and functions for model tuning. Users can also do the Monte-Carlo simulation. Various system properties e.g., response time, are also optimized using this tool.*
Symbolic math toolbox	*This toolbox helps in generating code for manipulation and graphical representation of the mathematical equations. It also supports the live editor to transform to Latex, HTML, etc.*
System identification toolbox	*This toolbox is widely used for parameter identification of linear and nonlinear systems. The major advantage of this toolbox is that it can operate in both the time and frequency domains.*
Text analytics toolbox	*This helps in analyzing the text report on social media, news feeds, surveys etc.*
UAV toolbox	*UAV toolbox has applications in UAV systems for modeling, simulation, and testing. These are also responsible for improving the compatibility of sensors with UAV systems.*
Wavelet toolbox	*Wavelet Toolbox is basically used for denoising the signal and images. It is also compatible with C/ C++/ CUDA code.*
WLAN toolbox	*This toolbox is used in the modeling and simulation of local are network communications systems. This toolbox also supports transceiving the RF signal from hardware.*

System composer	*It helps in analyzing the system model. It also supports live view of the model.*
Statistics and ML toolbox	*It gives the formulation to model the data. This also helps in creating numeric values for the Monte Carlo simulation.*
Simscape fluids	*This toolbox gives the model for the fluid system. The major advantage of this system is that it is compatible with mechanical systems, electrical systems, etc.*
Simscape electrical	*It helps to simulate several e.g., electrical, mechanical systems etc. It can be useful for developing control systems and electrical systems.*
Simscape driveline	*It has applications in modeling and simulation of rotational and translational mechanical systems. It is compatible with C programming.*
Robust control toolbox	*The uncertain model is generated using the robust control toolbox. It also helps to analyze the uncertainty in several systems. It reduces plant and controller order.*
Risk management toolbox	*This toolbox is used to model consumer and corporate credit risk. These are basically used for the probability default model.*
Radio Frequency toolbox	*RF toolbox helps to work with RF systems. It is also useful for both time-domain analysis and frequency domain analysis.*
Predictive maintenance	*It is helpful in detecting faults and estimating the remaining useful life of a mechanical system. It is also used for data management.*
Phased array system	*It has the application in direction-of-arrival (DOA), range-Doppler estimation. It is also useful in designing the waveform.*
Partial differential equation	*It helps in generating mathematical formulation of structure mechanical systems, heat transfer systems, electromagnetics, etc. Users can also do the postprocessing and visualization using this toolbox.*
Optimization toolbox	*This toolbox is used to optimize nonlinear systems. It is also useful for linear, quadratic programming, and several other mathematical formulations.*
Navigation toolbox	*It helps in modeling MAP representation (2-dimensional, 3-dimensional), SLAM, and path planning. It has applications in*

	sensor modeling, pose estimation using sensors, and navigation systems.

Due to the availability of these toolboxes, and comfortability for the users, MATLAB online is becoming popular with the users. Following are the merits of MATLAB online [9]:

- **Downloading and Installation not required:** *MATLAB online allows users to access MATLAB products using any standard web browser on any computer with an internet connection. Users need not download or install the MATLAB product, rather they can access it online by signing in to their MathWorks account.*
- **Collaboration for online sharing:** *Users can share the m-files, live scripts, and several other MATLAB products using MATLAB online. This enables the teachers to conduct the training program, webinars, seminars, etc., in a convenient manner.*
- **Latest MATLAB version:** *MathWorks provides the latest version of MATLAB to the users on MATLAB online platform. There is no need to update the license for the same.*
- **Cloud storage:** *MathWorks provides a 5GB MATLAB drive for storing and accessing the files which can be accessed online from anywhere or from any computer. This feature also enables the user to synchronize the files between the computer and MATLAB online. The users can also import and export the files from any computer to a MATLAB drive.*
- **Hardware interaction***: MATLAB online is compatible with USB webcams and audio playback devices using Google chrome. It can also interact with low-processing devices such as Raspberry Pi.*

MATLAB online allows the users to use the cloud solution e.g., MATLAB and Simulink online, MATLAB grader, ThingSpeak, MATLAB drive, etc. To access these facilities, users meet the system specifications or requirements which are mentioned as follows [10]:

- *The recommended browser is Google chrome. It is also compatible with cloud solutions that are adaptable with almost all modern web browsers e.g., Google Chrome, Mozilla Firefox, Apple Safari, and Microsoft Edge which runs on Windows, Linux, and Mac.*
- *In the browser setting, cookies, pop-ups, and JavaScript should be enabled.*
- *It requires a good speed broadband connection with a 1Mbps minimum speed.*
- *MATLAB is available on the system and MATLAB mobile for smart devices.*
- *The minimum screen resolution and memory required for MATLAB are 1024×768 and 2GB, respectively.*
- *It supports ThingSpeak where the IoT devices must reinforce HTTP, TCP/IP, and MQTT protocols. Moreover, the firewall should support the connection to the above-mentioned protocol.*
- *Several amalgamations with learning management networks need LTI1.1 or LTI1.3.*

Besides the advantages of MATLAB and Simulink online, these have several demerits also [8]. Some of these are enlisted below:

MATLAB online demerits: *MATLAB online is incompatible with some hardware e.g., instrument control. It does not support packaging tool for add-ons, MATLAB compiler,*

MATLAB compiler SDK, Windows component i.e., COM. Users can operate xlsread and xlswrite in basic mode only. The files with sizes larger than 256MB need to be operated through MATLAB drive. Beside these, MATLAB online does not fully support a graphical interface to the profiler, shell-escape bang (!) command. The app design facility can only be accessed using Google chrome and Microsoft edge.

Simulink online demerits:

Simulink online does not support variant manager and Simulink debugger. External mode is not available while communicating with raspberry pi hardware. Moreover, Simulink online does not support deployment when communicating with parrot mini drone hardware. Copy/paste feature from exterior applications is applicable. Simulink online is not compatible with screen resolutions higher than 1900×1200. Apart from the above limitations, the performance of Simulink online outside the United States is poor.

2.3.2 MATLAB offline

MATLAB offline works on the computer without internet connection. It is the most popular amongst MATLAB users worldwide. The main reason is its better compatibility with the hardware, accessibility of all MATLAB toolboxes, no dependency on the availability of internet connection, etc. Once the MATLAB products are installed on a computer (installation procedure is already discussed in Section 2.2), it is ready to use without an internet connection. The user needs the internet connection only for downloading the files and installing the product. MathWorks provides a network-based MATLAB license e.g., network concurrent which does not need an internet connection, rather it needs a connection to the license manager server on the local network for accessing the license. The following are the merits of MATLAB in offline version:

MATLAB offline merits*:*

- **Compatibility with the hardware:** *MATLAB offline is more compatible with hardware like Raspberry Pi, USB webcams, serialport(), playback devices etc. This is due to the availability of huge space for processing and independence to use without any web browsers.*
- **Better performance***: MATLAB offline gives better performance as it is independent of internet connection and online MATLAB server. The heavy file can easily be handled in the offline version.*
- **Support graphical interface:** *MATLAB offline supports a graphical interface to the profiler.*
- **More features to operate:** *MATLAB offline supports more features like better screen resolution, copy-paste from external applications, variant manager, Simulink debugger, etc.*

Due to the aforementioned advantages of the offline version of MATLAB, there are more than 4 million active users worldwide. Moreover, when compared to MATLAB online, MATLAB offline has several constraints. Some are as follows:

MATLAB offline demerits*:*

- *It requires downloading the product files, which need huge memory space. Installation is also a time-consuming process, though, it is a one-time process.*

- *Collaboration with the others is a bit complex in offline MATLAB and makes it more complex than MATLAB online.*
- *The latest version of MATLAB offline is not updated automatically unless the user buys the license of the latest one.*

Unit Summary

The following points summarise the unit:

- *History of MATLAB*

  - Inventor: Cleve Moler.

  - Developer: MathWorks.
- *Latest version R2022a was released in March 2022.*
- *Written in: C/C++, MATLAB*
- *Operating system: Windows, Linux, MacOS*
- *Editor window, command window, workspace window.*
- *Users can use the Help section to explore the toolboxes and MATLAB commands.*
- *MATLAB can be installed using: (i) standard installation method, and (ii) installation without using an internet connection.*
- *MATLAB can be accessed using : (i) online mode, and (ii) offline mode.*
- *MATLAB online was released in March 2017.*
- *MATLAB online has the following merits:*

  - no downloading and no installation,

  - collaboration for online sharing,

  - latest version available for the user,

  - cloud storage
- *Cloud solution support by MATLAB online:*

  - MATLAB and Simulink online

  - MATLAB grader
- *MATLAB online has the following demerits:*

  - Hardware incompatibility and graphical user interface not supported

  - Simulink online has constraints of performance, accessibility, and compatibility.
- *MATLAB offline has the advantage of*

  - better performance and compatibility with hardware

  - support several features, e.g., graphical user interface, etc.
- *Matlab offline has the following disadvantages*

  - Complex downloading and installation process

  - a collaboration with others not available,

  - latest version not available.

EXERCISES

Multiple Choice Questions

2.1 MATLAB was originally designed by

(a) Steve Bangert (b) Cleve Moler (c) John N. Little (d) John Little

2.2 MATLAB was commercially released in

(a) 1960 (b) 1974 (c) 1984 (d) 1979

2.3 ____________ developed the MATLAB software.

(a) MathWorks, Inc. (b) Microsoft (c) Google (d) None of these

2.4 MATLAB is available in

(a) Online version (b) Offline version (c) Both online and offline (d) None of these

2.5 MATLAB can be accessed using

(a) Windows (b) Mac (c) Linux (d) all of the above

2.6 In the standard installation method, MATLAB is installed on a computer using

(a) internet connection (b) without an internet connection.

(c) both, (a) and (b) (d) none of the above

2.7 In which year, MATLAB online was released?

(a) 1984 (b) 2017 (c) 2019 (d) 2014

2.8 Latest version of MATLAB, R2022a, was released in

(a) 2021 (b) 2022 (c) 2019 (d) 2020

2.9 How much is the cloud storage capacity of MATLAB drive?

(a) 5GB (b) 2GB (c) 3GB (d) 7GB

2.10 Which of the following is not the cloud solution provided by MATLAB online?

(a) ThingSpeak (b) MATLAB grader (c) MATLAB drive (d) MathWorks

2.11 What is the minimum memory of a computer required for a cloud solution?

(a) 5GB *(b) 2GB* *(c) 3GB* *(d) 1GB*

2.12 MATLAB online is incompatible with

(a) USB webcam *(b) Audio devices* *(c) Raspberry pi* *(d) instrument control*

2.13 Maximum screen resolution supported by Simulink online is

(a) 1900×1200 *(b) 2560×1440* *(c) 1080×600* *(d) 1280×720*

2.14 Which version of MATLAB supports the graphical interface?

(a) MATLAB online *(b) MATLAB offline* *(c) Both (a) and (b)* *(d) None of the above*

2.15 Statement 1: Latest version of MATLAB offline is updated automatically without getting the license of the latest version.

Statement 2: Latest version of MATLAB online is updated automatically without getting the license for the latest version.

(a) Only statement 1 is true.

(b) Only statement 2 is true.

(c) Both the statements, statement 1 and statement 2 are true.

(c) Both the statements, statement 1 and statement 2 are false.

Answers to Multiple Choice Questions
2.1 (b), 2.2 (c), 2.3 (a), 2.4 (c), 2.5 (d), 2.6 (a), 2.7 (b), 2.8 (b), 2.9 (a), 2.10 (d), 2.11 (b), 2.12 (d), 2.13 (a), 2.14 (b), 2.15 (b)

Short and Long Answer Type Questions

2.1 Write a short note on the following

(a) Command window

(b) Editor window

(c) Workspace

2.2 What are the advantages and disadvantages of MATLAB online.

2.3 What are the advantages and disadvantages of the offline version of MATLAB.

2.4 Briefly describe the prerequisite system requirements for the latest version of MATLAB.

2.5 *Compare the installation methods for installing MATLAB i.e., standard installation method and installation without using internet connection method.*

2.6. *Explain the significance of the workspace window.*

2.7 *Write a brief note on toolbox availability in MATLAB online and MATLAB offline.*

2.8 *Convert the background of the MATLAB layout such that the MATLAB environment is black and the font color is white.*

2.9 *How to clean the command history.*

2.10 *How to remove the content from the command window.*

2.11 *Try to resize the command window and editor window such that both windows take equal space.*

2.12 *Change the font and writing style of the editor window.*

2.13 *Write applications of the following toolboxes:*

- *(a) Signal processing toolbox*
- *(b) Control system toolbox*
- *(c) Image processing toolbox*
- *(d) Aerospace toolbox*

2.14 *Which are the supported browsers for cloud solutions in MATLAB online.*

2.15 *Write a short note on system requirements for using a cloud solution.*

Know More

Cleve Moler *is an American mathematician and computer programmer. He earned his graduate degree and doctorate degree from California Institute of Technology in 1961 and Stanford University in 1965, respectively. He developed numerical computing packages and gave these to his students. He is co-founder of MathWorks which then commercialized its product i.e., MATLAB and Simulink. Cleve Moler received the Computer Pioneer Award and IEEE John von Neumann Medal in 2012 and 2014, respectively.*

MathWorks: *MathWorks is a private corporation in America which handles computer software. MathWorks's headquarter is at Natick, Massachusetts, USA. Its major products are MATLAB and Simulink. Cleve Moler and Jack Little initially set up the company to provide free mathematical computing tools to graduate and post-graduate students in the 1970s. Later, Little and Steve Bangert did the programming in C language. Then, they (along with Cleve Moler) established MathWorks. Today, over 4 million active users are there worldwide.*

References

[1] *'About MATLAB', 2022. [Online]. Available: https://in.mathworks.com/products/matlab.html [Accessed: September- 2022].*

[2] *'About Simulink', 2022. [Online]. Available: https://in.mathworks.com/products/simulink.html [Accessed: September- 2022].*

[3] *'MATLAB Applications and Toolbox', 2022. [Online]. Available: https://in.mathworks.com/ [Accessed: September- 2022].*

[4] *'System Requirements for MATLAB', 2022. [Online]. Available: https://in.mathworks.com/support/requirements/matlab-system-requirements.html [Accessed: September- 2022].*

[5] *'Install Products', 2022. [Online]. Available: https://in.mathworks.com/help/install/install-products.html [Accessed: September- 2022].*

[6] *'Install Products Using Internet Connection', 2022. [Online]. Available: https://in.mathworks.com/help/install/ug/install-products-with-internet-connection.html [Accessed: September- 2022].*

[7] *'Install Products Using File Installation Key', 2022. [Online]. Available: https://in.mathworks.com/help/install/ug/install-using-a-file-installation-key.html [Accessed: September- 2022].*

[8] *'General Limitations in MATLAB online', 2022. [Online]. Available: https://in.mathworks.com/products/matlab-online/limitations.html [Accessed: September- 2022].*

[9] *'Merits of MATLAB online', 2022. [Online]. Available: https://in.mathworks.com/products/matlab-online.html [Accessed: September- 2022].*

[10] *'Browser Requirements', 2022. [Online]. Available: https://in.mathworks.com/support/requirements/browser-requirements.html [Accessed: September- 2022].*

3 Basics of MATLAB

UNIT SPECIFICS

This unit covers the following aspects:

- *Variables with their naming convention*
- *Operators in MATLAB which include arithmetic, relational and logical operators*
- *Rational expressions in MATLAB*
- *Type range and type casting in MATLAB*

This unit starts with the introduction to variables and their applications in MATLAB programming. It also explains the use of different operators in MATLAB with appropriate examples for each. Moreover, it considers the rational expressions and operation of these expressions using MATLAB. Besides these, it explains the different data types and their conversions. This unit contains selected information as 'Note' to discuss the key points of the content and exclusively covers a variety of examples and the discussion on them. A large variety of Multiple-Choice Questions (MCQs) with their solutions at the end of the unit are discussed. The MCQs are appended with short and long-type questions which have two different categories. It also enlisted references and recommended readings which helps the students to explore more about the content.

RATIONALE

This unit familiarizes the students with the variables and their significance in MATLAB. It explains several conventions for naming a variable. This unit also discusses the string and character array. Several mathematical computations of more than two operands are accomplished using the different operators. It helps the students to understand these operators, e.g., arithmetic, logical and relational operators. Moreover, it also clarifies the application of these operators which can be further used for engineering applications. This unit also introduces the rational expressions and their uses in MATLAB. This becomes useful for complex mathematical expressions. The simplification of the rational expressions leads to a decrease in the computational burden of the system. Besides these, it also discusses the different data types and their conversion using distinct MATLAB commands. Appended with this, the unit explains each topic with suitable examples having explanations of each example.

PRE-REQUISITES

MATLAB environment

Basic mathematical concepts

UNIT OUTCOMES

The outcomes of this unit are as follows:

U3-O1:MATLAB variables and their applications

U3-O2: Explain operators in MATLAB

U3-O3: Rational expressions in MATLAB

U3-O4: Type casting in MATLAB

Unit-3 Outcomes	EXPECTED MAPPING WITH COURSE OUTCOMES (1- Weak Correlation; 2- Medium correlation; 3- Strong Correlation)				
	CO-1	CO-2	CO-3	CO-4	CO-5
U3-O1	1	2	3	1	1
U3-O2	1	2	1	1	1
U3-O3	1	2	1	1	1
U3-O3	1	2	1	1	2

We have seen the history of MATLAB, gradual development of the MathWorks organization in the previous unit and explained how to install and work on MATLAB. Unit 2 also covered the details of command, editor, and workspace windows. The users can introduce the input in the editor window, or in the command window. The user gets spontaneous output using the command window. However, the editor window is preferred for long and complex MATLAB program statements. It saves MATLAB programs in m-files (with .m format) which can be accessed in the future. The aim of this unit is to introduce the variables and the basic operations, e.g., arithmetic, logical, relational, etc., with variables in MATLAB. This unit will cover the variables and operators of MATLAB. Next, it introduces the rational expressions in MATLAB. Finally, the type range and type casting will be discussed with examples.

3.1 Variables in MATLAB

MATLAB deals with the time-varying information or data obtained from the physical world e.g., gyroscope data, accelerometer data, etc. These data are in the form of numeric values, words, and so on. MATLAB has enormous mathematical functions and tools to execute the different operations on this physical world information. MathWorks has introduced a huge number of toolboxes to build up these functions. MATLAB uses variables for further processing of the data. This section introduces the variables and the basic variable types in MATLAB. A variable in the programming language is used to reserve some form of value. Using the variable in MATLAB helps to avoid repeating the same value frequently in the code and thus improves the readability of the script.

Different types of variables require unequal memory size which depends on the type of the values. MATLAB supports different types of values, such as Numeric (plain integer, long integer, float (real number), complex), Boolean (logical), or char (string). Let i *be a variable and* k *value assigned to it. In order to define a variable, the variable name always appear on the left of equality, i.e.,* $(variable = value) \Rightarrow (i = k)$.

Example: 3.1

Assign the numeric value 10 *to a variable* i.

Solution:

>> $i = 10$

$i =$

10

(Continue for error): *Assign the numeric value 10 to a variable* i.

Solution:

>> $10 = i$

$10 = i$

↑

Error: Incorrect use of '=' operator.

(Continue for using semicolon) : *Assign a numeric value* 10 *to variable* i.

Solution:

>> $i = 10;$

>>

Description of Example 3.1: *After typing* $i = 10$ *in the Command Window, as shown in Figure 3.1, the value* 10 *is assigned to the variable* i. *Typing* $i = 10$ *does not imply that variable* i *equals* 10. *The symbol "=" is known as an assignment operator in MATLAB. It is worth noting that the variable* i *is kept on the left side of the assignment operator else it leads to an error message as shown in Example 3.1 (Continue for error). The symbol ';' is put after the variable name to avoid hitting the enter key for displaying the content. It is also noted that the variable in MATLAB is an array or matrix. Example 3.1 creates a 1-by-1 matrix named* i *and the value* 10 *is assigned to* i.

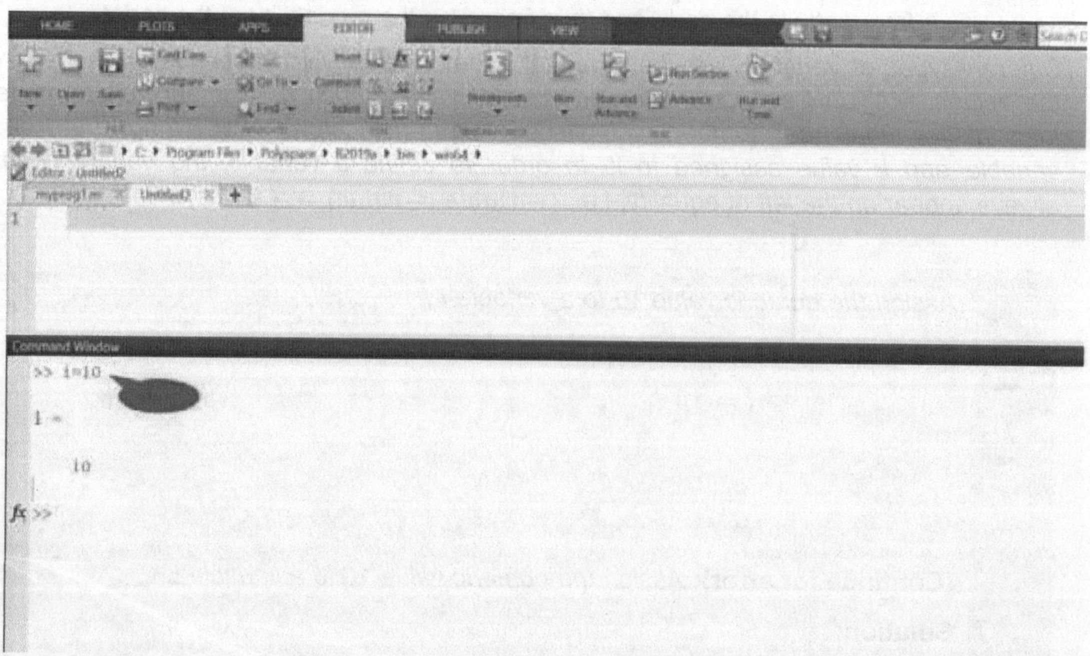

Figure 3.1: *Illustration of assigning value to variable using the command window.*

3.1.1 Variables naming conventions

Variable naming conventions in programming languages help to move easily from language to language. It also helps to communicate the source code from one developer to fellow developers. The most common variable naming conventions in MATLAB are as follows:

- *Variable names should begin with alphabets (lowercase or uppercase).*
- *Variable names support only the underscore symbol ('_') inside or at the end of the variable name.*
- *MATLAB is case-sensitive, so variables X and x are not the same.*
- *Keywords in a programming language are reserved for a specific purpose. The variable name in MATLAB should not be the same as the MATLAB keywords. The list of the MATLAB keywords, which can be found by running the built-in function iskeyword(), includes 'catch', 'classdef', 'spmd', 'elseif', 'end', 'for', 'function', 'global', 'if', 'else', 'otherwise', 'parfor', 'persistent', 'continue', 'return', 'switch', 'break', 'try', 'case' and 'while' [1]. MATLAB keywords are case-sensitive and have different meanings with upper and lower letters.*
- *The space is not allowed in variable name. Name with space will be considered as two different variables and give an error.*
- *MATLAB provides some predefined variables which cannot be used as variable names as they can create conflict with user-defined variable names [2]. Some predefined variables in MATLAB are as follows:*

  - **pi:** *It is a mathematical term* π.
  - **i or j:** *It represents the complex number which has the value* (-1).
  - **inf:** *Denotes the infinity value in MATLAB.*
  - **NaN:** *It indicates 'not a number'.*
  - **clock:** *Represents the time in MATLAB.*
  - **date:** *It shows the current date.*
  - **eps:** *It denotes 'epsilon', which is the smallest number in MATLAB.*
  - **ans:** *Shows the outcome in the command window.*

Example: 3.2

Assign values 10, 12, *and* 14 *to variables* i, i_7, *and* $i8$, *respectively.*

Solution:

$>> i = 10$

$i =$

10

```
>> i_7 = 12
   i_7 =
        12
```

```
>> i8 = 14
   i8 =
        14
```

(Continue for error): *Assign values* 10 *and* 12 *to variables* i# *and* i_7*, respectively.*
Solution:

```
>> i# = 10
   i# = 10
   Error: Invalid text character.
```

```
>> i_7 = 12
   i7
   Error: Undefined function or variable ' i7 '.
```

(Continue for error because of case-sensitive): *Assign value* 10 *to the variable i.*
Solution:

```
>> i = 10
   I =
   Error: Undefined function or variable ' I '.
```

(Continue for error because of using keyword): *Assign 10 and 12 to the variables k and K, respectively.*
Solution:

```
>> k = 10
   k
```

Error: Incorrect use of '=' operator.

>> $K = 10$

K

$= 10$

(Continue for error due to space): *Assign value 10 to the variable NEW DELHI.*

Solution:

>> $NEW\ DELHI = 10$

$NEW\ DELHI$

Error: Undefined function 'NEW' for input arguments of type 'char'.

Description of Example 3.2: *The assigned value 10 to i variable successfully works because i is an alphabet. The remaining part of the variable name is followed by underscore, numbers, and alphabets. Example 3.2 (Continue for error) illustrates an incorrect variable because the first convention of the variable name is not an alphabet. Next, $i\#$ gives an error because the variable name allows only underscore and other symbols are syntactically invalid. The variable I is an undefined variable as MATLAB is case-sensitive. Similarly, the variables i and I are treated as different variables. The variable k gives an error because it is a MATLAB keyword. However, K is not a keyword and can successfully work as a variable. The space in the variable name $NEW\ DELHI$ gives an error as MATLAB does not successfully recognize $[NEW$, space, $DELHI]$.*

3.1.2 Character variables

MATLAB supports character arrays and string arrays to represent the text. Character arrays are the succession of the characters and they basically used to accumulate fragments of texts as character vectors. These character arrays are represented using single quotes. It is also possible that the inputs of the arrays are different data types. In such cases, the char function (denoted as $char$) converts the array of different types into the character. $char()$ function also converts the multiple arrays into a single character array.

Example: 3.3

Store a character array Learnprogramming to a variable chr.

Solution:

```
>> chr = ('Learnprogramming')
chr =
```

```
'Learnprogramming'
```

Access information of variable chr.

Solution:

```
>> whos chr

   Name    Size    Byte    Class    Attributes

   chr     1×13    26      char
```

(Continue for concatenation): *Write a program to concatenate two character arrays.*

Solution:

```
>> chr1=('MAHARASHTRA');
>> chr2=(chr1, 'PUNE')
 chr2=
      'MAHARASHTRAPUNE'
```

(Continue to retrieve sequence from character array): *Store a character array MAHARASHTRA to a variable. Retrieve the sequence AHA from the array MAHARASHTRA.*

Solution:

```
>> chr1=('MAHARASHTRA');
>> chr1(2:4)
ans=
    'AHA'
```

Description of Example 3.3: *Former part of the example assigns the character 'Learnprogramming' to the variable chr. For this, the character array needs to be kept in single quotes (' '). The information in the character array can be accessed using whos command. whos command displays information in terms of name, size, memory storage, class, and attributes. The next part shows the concatenation of the two character arrays, 'MAHARASHTRA' and 'PUNE', to give the output character 'MAHARASHTRAPUNE'. MATLAB allows retrieving the sequence from the character array. The latter part of the example describes the method to retrieve 'AHA' from the character array 'MAHARASHTRA'.*

3.1.3 String variables

A string in MATLAB is a vector and its characters are the elements of the string. The sequence of characters is stored in terms of a data type called a string data type. Same as character data type, the user can designate the text in terms of the m-file name, graphical labels, and textual facts. In the string arrays, the text is confined in double-quotes (" ").

Example: 3.4

Store a string array to variable str.

Solution:

```
>> str=("Learn programming")
str =
    "Learn programming"
```

Access information of variable str.

Solution:

```
>> whos str
  Name    Size    Byte    Class    Attributes
  str     1 × 1   174     string
```

(Continue to convert a string into character): *Convert a string array "Learn programming" into a character array.*

Solution:

```
>> str=("Learn", "programming")
str =
    "Learn" "programming"
>> chr = convertStringsToChars(str)
chr =
    'Learn' 'programming'
```

(Combining text with string): *Compute the circumference of a circle of radius 2 unit.*

Solution:

```
>> Radius = 2;
>> Circumference = 2 ∗ pi ∗ Radius;
>> Statement = "Total circumference is" + Circumference + "unit"
Statement =
            "Total circumference is 12.5664 unit"
```

Description of Example 3.4: *In the first part of the example, it assigns the string "Learn programming" to the variable* `str`*. Further, the information about the* `str` *display using the* `whos` *command. The next part of the example uses convertStringsToChars( ) to convert the string array into a character array. Users can append text with strings using the '+' operator. The latter part of the example explains the application of '+' operator to add text with string.*

3.2 Operators in MATLAB

Operators are the mathematical functions that are used to accomplish the mathematical computation of two or more operands. As the operands can be numeric values, variables, or logical expressions, the operators are classified into different categories, e.g., arithmetic, relational, logical, etc. These mathematical operators take the mathematical expressions in the form of linear equations, differential equations, etc., as the input and give a corresponding output when executed in computer programming languages.

3.2.1 Arithmetic operators

Arithmetic operators are the mathematical functions that are used to perform different mathematical operations. The most commonly used operators in MATLAB are as shown in Table 3.1.

Table 3.1: *Commonly used arithmetic operators [3].*

Symbol	Definition	MATLAB function	Example	Output
+	*Addition*	*plus()*	4+2	6
-	*Subtraction*	*minus()*	4-2	2
*	*Multiplication*	*times()*	4*2	8
/	*Division*	*rdivide()*	4/2	2
^	*Exponentiation*	*power()*	4^2	16

Example: 3.5

Add two numbers and multiply them by a real number.
Solution:

```
>> x = 2; y = 3;
>> z = x + y;
z =
    5
>> m = 5*z;
m =
    25
```

(Continue using inbuilt MATLAB functions): *Using inbuilt MATLAB functions to solve the above example.*
Solution:

```
>> z = plus(x, y);
z =
    5
>> m=times(5, z);
m =
    25
```

Description of Example 3.5: *The example first assigns two numbers 2 and 3 to the variables x and y, respectively. Sum value of these two variables is assigned to another variable z. Further, the variable z is multiplied by the number 5 and the final result is assigned to a variable m. MATLAB has its own inbuilt functions to perform arithmetic operations. Table 3.1 illustrates these inbuilt mathematical functions. The use of plus() and times() are shown in the example.*

MATLAB is useful for complex mathematical computation. So, the use of parentheses becomes crucial for such complex expressions. When these parentheses are used, they are given the highest precedence for computation.

Example: 3.6

Compute 2 + 3 × 4 using MATLAB.
Solution:

```
>> 2+3*4
ans =
```

```
14
```

(Continue using parentheses): *Solve (2+3)×4 using MATLAB.*
Solution:

```
>> (2+3)*4;
ans =
     20
```

Discussion on Example 3.6: *The output of* $(2 + 3 \times 4)$ *is 14, on the other hand, the use of the parentheses* $(2 + 3) \times 4$ *leads to the outcome of 20. This is due to the fact that MATLAB works on a precedence basis. It gives the highest precedence to parentheses than another mathematical operator [4]. The order of preference for mathematical operators is shown in Table 3.2.*

Table 3.2: *Precedence of the operators and parentheses.*

Precedence	Operator/parentheses
Higher to lower priority order	• *Parentheses are computed with the highest priority.* • *The exponentials are given second priority and computed from left to right.* • *The multiplication/division is given third priority and computed from left to right.* • *Addition/subtraction are given the lowest precedence.*

Note: *MATLAB by default displays four digits after the decimal point. A user can change the number of such digits using the format command. format bank, format long, and format short commands are used to display two, fifteen, and four digits, respectively after the decimal point.*

Example: 3.7

Evaluate $2 * (4 + 2^3)/3 * (5 + 1)$ *expression.*
Solution:

```
>> 2 * (4 + 2 * 2 * 2)/3 * (5 + 1)
ans =
```

1.3333

(Continue for highly precise output): *Evaluate* $2 * (4 + 2^3)/3 * (5 + 1)$ *expression and display the output up to 15 digits.*
Solution:

```
>> format long

>> 2 * (4 + 2 * 2 * 2)/3 * (5 + 1)

ans =

    1.333333333333333
```

(Continue for moderate precise output):
Evaluate $2 * (4 + 2^3)/3 * (5 + 1)$ *and display the output up to 4 digits.*
Solution:

```
>> format short

>> 2 * (4 + 2 * 2 * 2)/3 * (5 + 1)

ans =

    1.3333
```

(Continue for low precise output): *Evaluate* $2 * (4 + 2^3)/3 * (5 + 1)$ *and display the output up to 2 digits.*
Solution:

```
>> format bank

>> 2 * (4 + 2 * 2 * 2)/3 * (5 + 1)

ans =

    1.33
```

Discussion on Example 3.7: *MATLAB displays the output in 4 digits after decimal point. The accuracy becomes crucial many times, thus, it requires more digits to express the results. For this, format long command can be used. format long command will increase the number of digits to 15 after the decimal point. Example shows the application of the format long command. It is clear that the format long command is useful if the user wants high accuracy in the results. format short command will lead to 4 digits after the decimal point. Moreover, format short command is useful when moderate accuracy is required. An extra number of bits at the outcome requires more memory space and it leads to an increase in processing time. In the long MATLAB programs, the* *aforementioned constraints become significant. Thus, the format bank command can be used to reduce the number of bits after decimal points. format bank command reduces the number of digits to two after the decimal place as shown in the example.*

Mathematical functions in MATLAB: *There are several mathematical functions given in MATLAB [5]. Users can give the input to these mathematical functions within the parentheses and MATLAB will give the corresponding output in terms of the numeric value or graphical representation. Some of the generally used inbuilt mathematical functions are mentioned in Table 3.3.*

Table 3.3: *Commonly used mathematical functions.*

Symbol	Definition	Example	Output
sin	Sine	$sin\ (pi/6)$	0.5000
cos	Cosine	$cos\ (pi/6)$	0.8660
tan	Tangent	$tan\ (pi/6)$	0.5774
exp	Exponential	$exp\ (1/2)$	1.6487
$log_e(.)$	Natural logarithm	$log_e(10)$	2.3026
$log_{10}(.)$	Logarithm with base 10	$log_{10}(10)$	1.0000
Square root	$(.)$	9	3.0000

Apart from the above mathematical functions, MATLAB has some other inbuilt mathematical representation. MATLAB gives the outcome of the expression $\frac{0}{0}$*, which is denoted by* NaN *(Not a number). For* $\frac{1}{0}$*, MATLAB gives* inf *(infinity) as output. Some of the mathematical representations available in MATLAB are illustrated in Table 3.4.*

Table 3.4: *Mathematical representation in MATLAB [4].*

Mathematical representation	Input command at prompt	Output
Infinity	$\frac{1}{0}$	*Inf*
Imaginary number	i	*1+1.0000i*
Not a number	$\frac{0}{0}$	*NaN*

π	*pi*	3.1416
Factorial (!)	factorial(3)	6

Note:

- *factorial (N) function in MATLAB works perfectly when* $N \leq 21$.
- *MATLAB identifies the inbuilt function 'i' as an imaginary number that has the value equal to* -1.

3.2.2 Relational operators

Relational operators compare the two expressions. The expressions can be represented in terms of the false statement (expressed as 0) or true statement (expressed as 1). Considering two variables x and y. The statement $x > y$ returns true if the value assigned to x is greater than the value assigned to y, otherwise, the statement returns false. For example, if the values assigned to x and y are 1 and 2, respectively. Then, the statement $x > y$ is false and returns 0 as the output command window. MATLAB also has relational functions to compare the mathematical expressions. Table 3.5 shows the relational operators and their corresponding MATLAB functions [6].

Table 3.5: *Relational operators and their corresponding MATLAB functions.*

Operators	Description	MATLAB function	Example	Output	Remark
>	greater than	$gt()$	$2 > 3$	0	False statement
>=	greater than or equal	$ge()$	$3 >= 2$	1	True statement
<	less than	$lt()$	$2 < 3$	1	True statement
<=	Less than or equal	$le()$	$3 <= 2$	0	False statement
~=	not equal	$ne()$	$2\sim = 3$	1	True statement
==	equal	$eq()$	$3 == 2$	0	False statement

Example: 3.8

Calculate 2 × (1 + 4) >= (2 + 8) using MATLAB.
Solution:

```
>> 2 * (1 + 4) >= (2 + 8)
```

```
ans =

      1
```

(Continue using MATLAB function): *Calculate 2 × (1 + 4) >= (2 + 8) using function ge( ).*

Solution:

```
>> ge(2 * (1 + 4), (2 + 8))

ans =

   1
```

Discussion on Example 3.8: *The statement is to compare the two expressions* $(2 \times (1 + 4))$ *and* $(2 + 8)$. *The condition of greater than or equal to is satisfied and the corresponding output is displayed as logical "1". MATLAB function ge() can also be used to compare the two expressions as shown in the example.*

Example: 3.9

Compute $(3^2) \sim= (1 + 2^4)$.

Solution:

```
>> 3 * 3 ~= (1 + 2 * 2 * 2* 2)

ans =

   1
```

(Continue using MATLAB function): *Calculate 2 × (1 + 4) ~= (2 + 8) using MATLAB function.*

Solution:

```
>> ne(2*(1+4), (2+8))

ans =

   0
```

Discussion on Example 3.9: *It compares the two mathematical expressions* 3^2 *and* $1 + 2^4$ *for the condition 'not equal to'. The output displays the logical "1" as the condition* *is satisfied. The second part of the example compares the expressions using the MATLAB function ne() for not equal to condition.*

3.2.3 Logical operators

Logical operators operate two logical statements or expressions. OR, AND, NOT are called fundamental logical operators. Apart from these three fundamental logical operators, there are other logical operators (called as universal logical operators), namely, EX-OR, EX-NOR. These other logical operators can be implemented from the fundamental logical operators. In MATLAB, the fundamental logical operators OR, AND, NOT are expressed as '|', '&', ' ~ ', respectively. The logical operators in MATLAB are shown in Table 3.6 [7].

Table 3.6: *Logical operators with their MATLAB functions.*

Logical operator	Symbol	MATLAB function	Example	Output
Logical OR	|	*and ()*	*1|0*	*1*
Logical AND	&	*and ()*	*1&0*	*0*
Logical NOT	~	*not ()*	*~ 1*	*0*
Logical OR (with short-circuiting)	||	——	*1||0*	*1*
Logical AND (with short-circuiting)	&&	——	*1&&0*	*0*

Consider A and B to be the two logical expressions. Table 3.7 illustrates OR, AND, NOT for different possible conditions of logical expressions A and B and corresponding logical output.

Table 3.7: *Truth table of logical operators [7].*

Expression ***A***	Expression ***B***	OR (|)	AND(&)	NOT ***A*** $(\sim A)$	NOT ***B*** $(\sim B)$
0	*0*	*0*	*0*	*1*	*1*
0	*1*	*1*	*0*	*1*	*0*
1	*0*	*1*	*0*	*0*	*1*
1	*1*	*1*	*1*	*0*	*0*

Note: *MATLAB provides the higher precedence for AND operation (&) as compared to OR operation (|). The computation takes place from left to right. For better results, use parentheses. Moreover, short-circuit AND (&&) and short-circuit OR (||) have the same order of precedence [3].*

Example: 3.10

Compute the output of the logical expression (Y OR NOT(Z)) AND (Y OR Z), where both expressions Y and Z are true.

Solution:

```
>> Y = 1;

>> Z = 1;

>> (Y||(~ Z))&&(Y||Z);

ans =

     1
```

(Continue for Y = 0, Z = 0): *Compute the output of the above expression when Y and Z are false.*

Solution:

```
>> Y = 0;

>> Z = 0;

>> (Y||(~ Z))&&(Y||Z);

ans =

     0
```

Discussion on Example 3.10: *Let* Y *and* Z*, both are true, i.e.,* $Y = 1$ *and* $Z = 1$*. The expression* $Y\ OR\ (NOT\ (Z))\ AND\ (Y\ OR\ Z)$ *can be expressed as* $1\ OR\ (NOT\ (1))\ AND\ (1\ OR\ 1)$*, which gives the result as logic '1'. In the latter part, both* Y *and* Z *are false. Therefore, the expression* $Y\ OR\ (NOT\ (Z))\ AND\ (Y\ OR\ Z)$ *results in* $0\ OR\ (NOT\ (0))\ AND\ (0\ OR\ 0)$*. Thus the output is finally logic "0".*

3.3 Rational expressions in MATLAB

A rational number expresses the ratio of two numbers i.e., $\frac{p}{q}$, where p and q are the integers and q is not equal to zero. MATLAB has a command, simplifyfraction(expr), to simplify the rational expressions. The common terms in numerator and denominator are excluded in the command. Another command, simplifyFraction(expr, 'Expand', true), expands the numerator and denominator in simplified forms.

Example: 3.11

Write a MATLAB program to simplify the expression $\frac{z \times (y^2 - 1)}{(y+1)(y-1)}$.

Solution:

```
>> syms y, z
>> Var1 = z*(y^2-1)/(y+1)*(y-1);
>> simplifyFraction(Var1)
ans =
z
```

Description of Example 3.11: *Symbols y and z are initialized by using syms y, z command. Next, assign the expression $\frac{z \times (y^2-1)}{(y+1)(y-1)}$ to a variable 'Var1'. Command simplifyFraction simplifies the expression $\frac{z \times (y^2 - 1)}{(y+1)(y-1)} = \frac{z\,(y+1)(y-1)}{(y+1)(y-1)}$ to z.*

Commands rat and $rat(\cdot)$ determine the rational approximation of the expression. The approximated values are in the form of an array that has the reduced version of the fraction extension. It is often preferable to express the floating numbers as rational numbers with numerators and denominators. rat command returns the approximate value of the variable in the form of $\frac{P}{Q}$. Similarly, the $rat(\cdot)$ command gives the approximate value of the variable in the following form of $Q_1 + \frac{1}{Q_2 + \frac{1}{Q_3 + \cdots + \frac{1}{Q_n}}}$, where Q_1, Q_2, …, Q_n are integers.

Example: 3.12

(π in terms of rational numbers):

Display the approximate value of π in terms of rational numbers.

Solution:

```
>> format rat
```

```
>> pi

ans =

        355/113
```

(π in terms of continued fraction expansion):
Display the approximate value of π in terms of continued fraction expansion.
Solution:

```
>> p = rat (pi);

p =

        '3 + 1/(7 + 1/(16))'
```

Description on Example 3.12: *The example illustrates the value of π in terms of rational numbers. By using rat command, it gives in the form of $\frac{P}{Q}$. Using command rat(.) for representing the value of π in continued fraction expression.*

Extracting numerator and denominator from the rational expression: *MATLAB uses numden function to draw out the numerator and denominator from a given symbolic number, expression, function, vector, or matrix expression.*

Example: 3.13

Extract the numerator and denominator from number $\frac{1}{4}$.

Solution:

```
>> [p, q] = numden(sym(1 / 4))

p = 1

q = 4
```

(Continue for expression): *Extract the numerator and denominator from rational expression $\frac{y-z}{(y^2+z^2)}$.*

Solution:

```
>> syms y z

>> [p, q] = numden(y-z) / (y^2+z^2)

p = y - z
```

q = y^2 + z^2

(Continue for function): *Consider the functions* $f(z) = \frac{e^z}{z^3}$ *and* $g(z) = \frac{\sin(z)}{z^2}$. *Extract the numerator and denominator from* $f(z)$ *and* $\frac{f}{g}$.

Solution:

```
>> syms f(z) g(z)
>> f(z) = exp(z) / z^3;
>> g(z) = sin(z) / z^2;
>> [p, q] = numden (f);
p(z) = exp(z)
q(z) = z^3
>> [p, q] = numden (f / g);
p(z) = exp(z)
q(z) = z*sin(z)
```

(Continue for rational expression): *Extract the numerator and denominator from transformed rational expression* $\left(\frac{y^2}{z}, \frac{z^2}{y}\right)$.

Solution:

```
>> [p, q] = numden(y^2 / z + z^2 / y)
p = y^3 + z^3
q = y * z
```

Discussion on Example 3.13: *It separates numerator and denominator from expressions* sym($\frac{1}{4}$) , $\frac{y-z}{(y^2+z^2)}$ *using the numden command. In the next part, the numerator and denominator are separated from the expression* $\frac{f}{g}$, *where* $f(z) = \frac{e^z}{z^3}$ *and* $g(z) = \frac{\sin(z)}{z^2}$. *The function numden transforms the numerator and denominator into one rational form such that the greatest common factor is equal to 1.*

3.4 Type range and type casting

As we have seen in the previous sections, MATLAB supports different data types. Table 3.8 summaries the data types and specifications [8]. It shows that each data type has a fixed format and utility. Using the proper data type helps to simplify the program. Furthermore, Table 3.9 gives the range of the numeric data type [9].

Table 3.8: *Illustration of data types in MATLAB.*

Data type	Significance
Numeric types	*Integer values, floating-point numbers, etc. are included*
Characters and strings	*These include text in terms of character and string arrays*
Date and time	*It shows date and time arrays in distinct representations*
Categorical arrays	*It contains qualitative data arrays, e.g., finite impulse response data*
Tables	*Tabular arrays include numerical or categorical data*
Timetables	*It includes time-stamped data in tabular representation*
Structures	*Structures contain arrays of different sizes and types*
Cell arrays	*Cell arrays include arrays of different sizes and types*
Functional handles	*It allows a variable for a functional call when required*
Map containers	*It contains different keys which are assigned with different values*
Time series	*It includes time-sampled data*
Data type identification	*These data types assist to identify the variable*
Data type conversion	*It leads to the conversion of data type to another data type*

Table 3.9: *Illustration of the details of numeric data types in MATLAB.*

Class	Storage	Range	Description
int8	*1 byte*	$[-2^{7}, 2^{7}-1]$	*8-bit signed integer arrays*

int16	2 byte	$[-2^{15}, 2^{15}-1]$	16-bit signed integer arrays
int32	4 byte	$[-2^{31}, 2^{31}-1]$	32-bit signed integer arrays
int64	8 byte	$[-2^{63}, 2^{63}-1]$	64-bit signed integer arrays
uint8	1 byte	$[0, 2^{8}-1]$	8-bit signed integer arrays
uint16	2 byte	$[0, 2^{16}-1]$	16-bit signed integer arrays
uint32	4 byte	$[0, 2^{32}-1]$	32-bit signed integer arrays
uint64	8 byte	$[0, 2^{64}-1]$	64-bit signed integer arrays

Type casting is used to change an expression from one data type to another. It helps to perform the operations effectively. For example, type casting converts a floating value into an integer value. This section covers the transformation of one data type to another. To convert a given data type of a variable into the desired data type, MATLAB uses typecast() command.

Example: 3.14

Convert $uint8(31)$ *and* $unit8(255)$ *into* $int(8)$.

Solution:

```
>> typecast(uint8(31),'int8')

ans =

      31

>> typecast(uint8(255),'int8')

ans =

      - 1
```

(Continue for vector) *Convert* $uint32([256 \quad 31 \quad 1])$ *vector into* $int(8)$.

Solution:

```
>> Z = uint32([256   31   1])

>> typecast(Z, 'int8 ')

ans =
```

```
1   0   0   0  31   0   0   0   1   0   0   0
```

Discussion on Example 3.14: *It converts* uint8(31) *and* unit8(255) *to* int(8) *data type using* typecast() *command. Then, for 'Continue for vector', the first element of Z is exceeding 8-bits. Thus, it is transformed from Z(9) to Z(10) as an overflow. It should be noted that each bit in uint32 is represented as 4 bits. Therefore, the total length in uint8 will be four times the length of uint32.*

The data type can also be classified as a single-precision array and double-precision array, on the basis of the number of digits required to express a floating-point number. Single precision arrays have applications where it requires low accuracy whereas double precision arrays have applications in scientific calculations where high accuracy is required. Single precision arrays are 32-bit floating-point values. Users can convert a given data type to a single-precision data type using the single(·) *command. Further, the information can be extracted from the variable using the* whos *command. MATLAB uses 'double precision' data type to store 64-bit floating-point values. Double-precision is the default data type if the data type of a given variable is not defined. Double precision variables can be either created by using* double(·) *or putting the data in a square bracket, i.e., '[ ]'.*

Example: 3.15

Represent a numerical value using a single-precision array, and extract the information of the variable.

Solution:

```
>> x = single(2);
>> whos x

Name        Size        Byte        Class        Attributes

x           1×1         4           single
```

Represent a numerical value using a double-precision array, and extract the information about the variable.

Solution:

```
>> x = 2;

>> whos x

Name        Size        Byte        Class        Attributes

x           1×1         8           double
```

Description of Example 3.15: *Initially, It assigns single-precision value 2 to the variable 'x' by using single(2) command. Then, it uses whos command to extract the information in terms of name, size, byte, class, and attributes about the variable 'x'. Continuing the example for double-precision value. The numerical value '2' is assigned to the variable 'x'. The default data type is a double data type associated with the variable 'x'.*

Unit Summary

Following points summarize the unit:

- *Variables reserve the values in different forms to avoid repetition in the program.*
- *MATLAB supports character arrays and string arrays to represent the text.*

  - In character arrays, the text is confined to single quotes.

  - In string arrays, the text is represented in double-quotes.
- *MATLAB operators are used to accomplish the mathematical computation of two or more operands.*
- *MATLAB operators include arithmetic operators, relational operators, logical operators, etc.*

  - Arithmetic operators include addition, subtraction, division, multiplication, and perform different mathematical operations.

  - Relational operators compare the two expressions. Relational operators include >, >=, <, <=, ~=, = =.

  - Logical operators operate the two logical statements or expressions. The fundamental logical operators are

  - OR (|),

  - AND (&),

  - NOT (~).
- *A rational number expresses the ratio of two numbers i.e.,* $\frac{p}{q}$*, where* p *and* q *are the integers and* q *is a non-zero value.*
- *numden command in MATLAB can be used to draw out the numerator and denominator from a given rational expression.*
- *Data type decides the properties associated with the numerical and character values.*

  - Data types include Numeric types, Characters, and strings, Date and time, Categorical arrays, Tables, Timetables, Structures, Cell arrays, Functional handles, Map containers, Time series, Data type identification, and Data type conversion.

  - Numeric data types include int8, int16, int32, int64, uint8, uint16, uint32, uint64.

- *Single precision arrays and double precision arrays represent the floating-point numbers to denote the number of bits after the decimal point.*

EXERCISES

Multiple Choice Questions

3.1 Correct way of assigning a numerical value '20' to a variable 'i'.

(a) >> i=20 *(b) >> 20=i* *(c) Both (a) and (b)* *(d) None of these*

3.2 Which of the following is the correct variable name?

(a) 22i *(b) I_2* *(c) for* *(d) None of these*

3.3 Which of the following is the correct variable name?

(a) if *(b) IF* *(c) 2IF* *(d) 2_IF*

3.4 The correct variable name is

(a) spmd *(b) switch* *(c) Try* *(d) try*

3.5 Which of the following is a predefined variable name?

(a) inf *(b) NaN* *(c) clock* *(d) All of above*

3.6 Which is not a predefined variable name?

(a) ans *(b) eps* *(c). data* *(d) date*

3.7 Which of the following is not a MATLAB keyword name?

(a) through *(b) case* *(c) catch* *(d) continue*

3.8 Which of the following is a MATLAB keyword name?

(a) for *(b) function* *(c). global* *(d) All of the above*

3.9 Which MATLAB command is used to extract the information about a variable?

(a) whose *(b) whos* *(c) Whos* *(d) Whose*

3.10 whos command in MATLAB gives the information about the variable in terms of

(a) Name, Size, Byte, Class, Attributes
(b) Name, Length, Byte, Class, Attributes
(c) Name, Size, Byte, Keywords, Attributes
(d) Name, Size, Byte, Class, Character

3.11 In the string arrays, the text is confined in ____________

(a) single-quotes *(b) double-quotes* *(c) Both (a) and (b)* *(d) None of these*

3.12 In the character arrays, the text is confined in ____________

(a) single-quotes *(b) double-quotes* *(c) Both (a) and (b)* *(d) None of these*

3.13 In MATLAB, which operators are given highest priority?

(a) Addition *(b) Multiplication* *(c) All parentheses* *(d) Subtraction*

3.14 Compute the output of the MATLAB statement

```
>> 5+4*2
```

(a) 18 *(b) 13* *(c) 9* *(d) None of these*

3.15 Compute the output of the MATLAB statement

```
>> (5+4/2)*2
```

(a) 14 *(b) 9* *(c) 12* *(d) 16*

3.16 Compute the output of the MATLAB statement

>> format bank

*>> 4 * (2 + 3 ^ 3)/3 * (7 + 1)*

(a) 309.33 *(b) 309.3333* *(c) 309.00* *(d) 309.33333333*

3.17 Compute the output of the MATLAB statement

>> format short

*>> 4 * (2 + 3 ^ 3)/3 * (7 + 1)*

(a) 309.33 *(b) 309.3300* *(c) 309.0000* *(d) 309.3333*

3.18 Compute the output of the MATLAB statement

*>> 4 * (2 + 3 ^ 3)>=44*

(a) 1 *(b) 0* *(c) NaN* *(d) Inf*

3.19 Compute the output of the MATLAB statement

*>> 2 * (1 + 2 ^ 2) ~ = 10*

(a) 1 *(b) 0* *(c) NaN* *(d) Inf*

3.20 Compute the output of the MATLAB statement

*>> eq(2 * (1 + 2 ^ 2) , 10)*

(a) 1 *(b) 0* *(c) NaN* *(d) Inf*

3.21 MATLAB function for '>=' is

(a) gte() *(b) get()* *(c) ge()* *(d) gt()*

3.22 Compute the output for the expression (A OR NOT(B)) AND (A OR B), if A is true, and B is false.

(a) 1 *(b) 0* *(c) NaN* *(d) Inf*

3.23 Compute the output for the expression (A OR NOT(B)) AND (A OR B), if A is false, and B is true.

(a) 1 *(b) 0* *(c) NaN* *(d) Inf*

3.24 What is the range of int16 data type?

(a) $[-2^7, 2^7 - 1]$ *(b)* $[-2^{15}, 2^{15} - 1]$ *(c)* $[-2^{31}, 2^{31} - 1]$ *(d)* $[-2^{63}, 2^{63} - 1]$

3.25 What is the range of uint32 data type?

(a) $[0, 2^8 - 1]$ *(b)* $[0, 2^{16} - 1]$ *(c)* $[0, 2^{32} - 1]$ *(d)* $[0, 2^{64} - 1]$

Answers to Multiple Choice Questions
3.1 (a), 3.2 (b), 3.3 (b), 3.4 (c), 3.5 (d), 3.6 (c), 3.7 (a), 3.8 (d), 3.9 (b), 3.10 (a), 3.11 (b), 3.12 (a), 3.13 (c), 3.14 (b), 3.15 (a), 3.16 (a), 3.17 (d), 3.18 (a), 3.19 (b), 3.20 (a),

3.21 (c), 3.22 (a), 3.23 (b), 3.24 (b), 3.25 (c)

Short and Long Answer Type Questions

Category-I

3.1 *What is a variable? Explain the variable naming conventions in MATLAB.*

3.2 *Enlist the predefined variables in MATLAB. Describe the significance of each in MATLAB programming.*

3.3 *Differentiate between the character array and string array.*

3.4 *Explain how concatenation of two-character arrays is done using MATLAB?*

3.5 *What is the significance of whos command in MATLAB? Explain with an example.*

3.6 *What are the operators in MATLAB. Write a short note on*

(a) arithmetic operators,

(b) logical operators,

(c) relational operators.

3.7 *Explain the order of preference for mathematical operators in MATLAB with an example.*

3.8 *Explain the significance of the following format commands with example*

(a) format long

(b) format short

(c) format bank

3.9 *Write a brief note on the following logical operators*

(a) OR

(b) AND

(c) NOT

3.10 *Write a short note on the data types.*

Category-II

3.11 *Assign the values 2, 4 and 6 to the variables x, x2 and x_2, respectively.*

3.12 *Retrieve the sequence 'hi' from the character array 'Delhi' using MATLAB*

3.13 *Compute the output of the expression* $8 \times (3 + 4^3) >= (1 + 2^3)/3 \times 4$ *in MATLAB and display the result with 15 digits after the decimal point.*

3.14 *Compute the output of the expression* $8 \times (3 + 4^3) >= (1 + 2^3)/3 \times 4$ *in MATLAB and display the result with 2 digits after the decimal point.*

3.15 *Find the output of the logical expression* $4 \times (2 + 3^2) >= (1 + 2^3)$ *using MATLAB.*

3.16 *Design an EX_OR operator using MATLAB.*

3.17 *Design an EX_NOR operator using MATLAB.*

3.18 *Extract the numerator and denominator from the expression* $\frac{x \times sin(x)}{e^{-3x} cos(x)}$ *using MATLAB.*

3.19 *Write a MATLAB program to convert the* $uint16(31)$ *and* $unit16(255)$ *to* $int(16)$ *data type. What conclusions can be drawn from the results?*

3.20 *Assign a numeric value to a variable. Extract the information about variables in MATLAB. Convert the default data type to a single-precision data type.*

References

[1] *'List of MATLAB keywords', 2022. [Online]. Available: https://www.mathworks.com/help/matlab/ref/iskeyword.html [Accessed: September- 2022].*

[2] *'Predefined values and variables in MATLAB', 2022. [Online]. Available: https://www.cdslab.org/matlab/notes/values-variables-types/variables/index.html [Accessed: September- 2022].*

[3] *'MATLAB Operators and Special Characters', 2022. [Online]. Available:*

https://www.mathworks.com/help/matlab/matlab_prog/matlab-operators-and-special-characters.html [Accessed: September- 2022].

[4] *'Operator Precedence', 2022. [Online]. Available: https://in.mathworks.com/help/matlab/matlab_prog/operator-precedence.html [Accessed: September- 2022].*

[5] *'Mathematical Functions', 2022. [Online]. Available: https://in.mathworks.com/help/symbolic/mathematical-functions.html [Accessed: September- 2022].*

[6] *'Relational Operators', 2022. [Online]. Available: https://in.mathworks.com/help/matlab/matlab_prog/array-comparison-with-relational-operators.html [Accessed: September- 2022].*

[7] *'Logical Operations', 2022. [Online]. Available: https://in.mathworks.com/help/matlab/logical-operations.html [Accessed: September- 2022].*

[8] *'Data Types', 2022. [Online]. Available: https://in.mathworks.com/help/matlab/data-types.html [Accessed: September- 2022].*

[9] *'Numeric Data Types with range', 2022. [Online]. Available: https://in.mathworks.com/help/matlab/numeric-types.html [Accessed: September- 2022].*

4 Vectors and Matrices in MATLAB

UNIT SPECIFICS

This unit discusses the following aspects:

- *Introduction to vectors and matrices*
- *Generation of different types of vectors and matrices in MATLAB*
- *Performing operations, arithmetic, relational and logic with vectors and matrices*

This unit covers the generation of vectors and matrices in MATLAB and their operations, including arithmetic, logical and relational operations. Each topic consists of various examples with a brief discussion on each example, which helps the readers get more into the content. This also discusses the sequence generation in MATLAB, which helps students use them in different applications, including signal generation in signal processing, control systems, etc.

This unit consists of various questions following Bloom's taxonomy's lower and higher order. These questions are in the form of multiple-choice and short and long answer questions. These questions help develop logical skills and understanding of the content. This unit also consists of experiments which are based on the applications of the content. These will help students to apply the concepts on real world problems. It also enlisted references and recommended readings which helps the students to explore more about the content.

RATIONALE

This unit familiarizes the students with vectors and matrices in MATLAB. Initially, it discusses the generation of sort of vectors and matrices appended with examples. Then, it covers different operations on vectors and matrices, including arithmetic operations, relational operations, and logical operations. Arithmetic operation includes addition, subtraction, multiplication division, and computation of power of the array. In relational operation, it compares the two expressions in the form of vectors or matrices. Logical operation includes the AND, OR, or NOT operations of the two or more expressions. These operations are crucial for engineering applications, applied mathematics, digital systems, etc. It also includes sequence generation which is helpful in time-varying signal generation, digital circuits, etc.

PRE-REQUISITES

Basics of linear algebra

Operators in MATLAB

Rational expressions in MATLAB

Type range and type casting in MATLAB

UNIT OUTCOMES

List of outcomes of this unit is as follows:

U4-O1: Create vector and matrices in MATLAB

U4-O2: Perform arithmetic, logical, and relational operations with vector and matrices

U4-O3: Generate sequence in MATLAB

Unit-4 Outcomes	EXPECTED MAPPING WITH COURSE OUTCOMES (1- Weak Correlation; 2- Medium correlation; 3- Strong Correlation)				
	CO-1	CO-2	CO-3	CO-4	CO-5
U4-O1	-	3	1	1	-
U4-O2	-	3	1	1	-
U4-O3	-	3	1	1	-

This unit covers the generation of vectors and matrices in MATLAB and their operations. Vectors and matrices are used to store the data. Vectors represent either in terms of rows or columns. A row vector with i elements has the dimension of $1 \times i$, and is expressed as $[\,\cdot\,]_{1\times i}$ Similarly, the column vector has the dimension $j \times 1$ and it can be represented as $[\,\cdot\,]_{j\times 1}$. A single-valued vector (scalar) has the number of rows and columns equal to unity, thus, it has the dimension of 1×1. Matrix represents a rectangular array of numbers, expressions, or symbols. The matrix consists of rows and columns. Consider a matrix F that has the dimension of $i \times j$, i.e. $[F]_{i\times j}$, in which i and j denote the number of rows and columns, respectively.

4.1 Vectors

The array of m-elements can be expressed as $\mathbb{R}m = (a_1, a_2 \cdots a_m)$. The elements in row vector and column vectors are horizontally and vertically expressed, respectively. Transpose of a row vector converts it into a column vector and vice versa. Transpose of a vector v is represented as v'. The element values in the zero vector are equal to zero. Vector allows the operations, e.g., arithmetic, logical, etc. However, arithmetic operations have to satisfy the dimensionality rule.

4.1.1 Create row and column vectors

Row vectors are created by putting all elements in a square bracket. The elements are separated by using the space bar or comma.

Example: 4.1

Generate a row vector of four elements using the spacebar.

Solution:

```
>> r = [1 2 3 4]

r =

     1   2   3   4
```

Generate a row vector of four elements using commas.

Solution:

```
>> r = [1, 2, 3, 4]

r =
```

```
1   2   3   4
```

Description of Example 4.1: *The row vector r consists of 4 elements that are separated by space. It can also be generated by using commas.*

A column vector is created by putting all the elements in a square bracket. Each element is separated by a semicolon.

Example: 4.2

Generate a column vector $\begin{bmatrix} 2 \\ 1 \\ 2 \\ 1 \end{bmatrix}$.

Solution:

```
>> c = [2; 1; 2; 1]

c = 2

    1

    2

    1
```

What is the output of two times transpose of vector $[1 \quad 2 \quad 3 \quad 4]$.

Solution:

```
>> c = [1 2 3 4]'

c = 1

    2

    3

    4
c' = 1  2  3  4
```

Discussion of Example 4.2: *It illustrates a column vector 'c ' of 4 elements separated by semicolon (;). Transpose to transpose of a vector generates the same vector because a row vector converts to a column vector by taking the transpose and again column vector to the row vector.*

4.1.2 Operation with vectors

This section discusses the arithmetic, relational, and logical operations with vectors.

SCAN ME
for more about array and matrix operation

(a) Arithmetic operation with vectors: *Vector addition follows the basic arithmetic formulation i.e., it allows the element-wise addition or subtraction. For element-wise arithmetic operation, the dimension of the vector should be matched. Consider two-row vectors* $r1 = [\ \cdot\ ]_{1\times m}$ *and* $r2 = [\ \cdot\ ]_{1\times n}$. *Then, the vector* $r1$ *can be added to the vector* $r2$ *if* m *and* n *are equal.*

Example: 4.3

Add the two vectors $[2 \quad 1 \quad 3 \quad 2]$ *and* $[2 \quad 2 \quad 3 \quad 3]$.

Solution:

```
>> r1 = [2  1  3  2];
>> r2 = [2  2  3  3];
>> r1 + r2
ans =
    4  3  6  5
```

(Continue with error): *Add the two vectors* $[2\ 1\ 3\ 2]$ and $[3\ 2\ 3]$.

Solution:

```
>> r1 = [2 1 3 2]
>> r3 = [3 2 2]
>> r1 + r3
r1 + r3
```

"Error: Matrix dimensions must agree".

Discussion of Example 4.3: *In the aforementioned example, the vectors* $r1$ *and* $r2$ *have the dimension* 1×4, *thus they are successfully added, and the output vector is* 1×4 *dimension. When the row vector* $r3 = [3 \quad 2 \quad 2]$ *of dimension* 1×3 *is added with* $r1$ *in MATLAB, it gives an error "Matrix dimensions must agree" as shown in the example.*

MATLAB supports scalar to vector and vector to vector multiplications. The scalar term in scalar to vector multiplication is multiplied with each element of a vector. Considering a scalar quantity α *and a vector* $r1$*, the result of scalar to vector multiplication is* $\alpha r1$*. Vector to vector multiplication requires the matching of the dimensions of vectors. Vector multiplication follows the element-wise multiplication where a row vector is multiplied with a row vector and column vector is multiplied with a column vector. For element-wise multiplication, ' .* ' must be used.*

A column vector can also be multiplied with the row vector. In this case, it can be done in two ways:

- *Dot product or inner product: When the product of vectors leads to a scalar value, it is called a dot product of vectors. If* x *and* y *are the two vectors then* $x \cdot y$ *denotes the dot product of two vectors. MATLAB function for the dot product is denoted by* $dot(x, y)$.
- *Outer product: When the product of vectors results in the formation of a matrix, then it is known as the outer product of vectors. For the two vectors* x *and* y*, Symbol* $x \otimes y$ *denotes the outer product of the two vectors.* $mtimes(x, y)$ *denotes the MATLAB function for the outer product of vectors.*

Example: 4.4

Multiply a vector $[1 \quad 2 \quad 3 \quad 4 \quad 5]$ *with a scaler* $\alpha = 5$.

Solution:

```
>> r1 = [1  2  3  4  5]

>> α = 5

>> α * r1

ans =

      5   10   15   20   25
```

(Distributive property in vectors): *Generate two vectors* $[1 \quad 2 \quad 3 \quad 4 \quad 5]$ *and* $[6 \quad 7 \quad 8 \quad 9 \quad 10]$. *Add the vectors and multiply them with a scaler* $\alpha = 5$.

Solution:

```
>> r1 = [1  2  3  4  5];

>> r2 = [6  7  8  9  10];

>> α = 5;

>> α * (r1 + r2)
```

$ans =$

$35 \quad 45 \quad 55 \quad 65 \quad 75$

$>> \alpha * r1 + \alpha * r2$

$ans =$

$35 \quad 45 \quad 55 \quad 65 \quad 75$

Discussion of Example 4.4: *Initially generates two vectors* $r1 = [1 \quad 2 \quad 3 \quad 4 \quad 5]$ *and* $r2 = [6 \quad 7 \quad 8 \quad 9 \quad 10]$. *The two vectors are added and the output is multiplied with a scalar 5. Scalar multiplication follows the distributive property, which states that* $\alpha * (r1 + r2) = \alpha * r1 + \alpha * r2$. *The example also illustrates the applicability of distributive property using MATLAB.*

Example: 4.5

(Multiplication of row vectors and scalar value): *Let two vectors are* $[3 \quad 4 \quad 1]$ *and* $[1 \quad 4 \quad 2]$. *Multiply the vectors and scale them by 2.*

Solution:

$>> r1 = [3 \quad 4 \quad 1];$

$>> r2 = [1 \quad 4 \quad 2];$

$>> \alpha = 2;$

$>> \alpha * r1 .* r2$

$ans =$

$6 \quad 32 \quad 4$

(Multiplication of column vectors and scalar value): *Let two vectors are* $[3 \quad 4 \quad 1]^T$ *and* $[1 \quad 4 \quad 2]^T$. *Multiply the vectors and scale them by 2.*

Solution:

$>> r1 = [3 \quad 4 \quad 1]';$

$>> r2 = [1 \quad 4 \quad 2]';$

$>> \alpha = 2;$

$>> \alpha * r1 .* r2$

ans =

6

32

4

(Inner product): *Compute the output of the following expression*

$$[3 \quad 4 \quad 1] \cdot [1 \quad 4 \quad 2]^T$$

Solution:

```
>> [3, 4, 1] *[1; 4; 2];
ans =
    21
```

(Outer product): *Compute the output of the following expression*

$$[3 \quad 4 \quad 1]^T \otimes [1 \quad 4 \quad 2]$$

Solution: >> [3; 4; 1] *[1, 4, 2]

```
ans=
    3  12  6
    4  16  8
    1   4  2
```

(Outer product using MATLAB function): *Compute the output of the following expression using MATLAB function*

$$[3 \quad 4 \quad 1]^T \otimes [1 \quad 4 \quad 2]$$

Solution: >> *mtimes*([3; 4; 1]', [1, 4, 2])

```
ans=
    3  12  6
    4  18  8
    1   4  2
```

Description of Example 4.5: *The two vectors* $r1 = [3 \quad 4 \quad 1]$ *and* $r2 = [1 \quad 4 \quad 2]$ *are multiplied to give output* $[3 \quad 16 \quad 2]$. *Then the scalar parameter* $\alpha = 2$ *is multiplied to the output and gives the final output vector* $[6 \quad 32 \quad 4]$. *Similarly, it multiplies the column* *vectors* $[3 \quad 4 \quad 1]^T$ *and* $[1 \quad 4 \quad 2]^T$ *using element-wise multiplication and gives the output* $[3 \quad 16 \quad 2]^T$. *It computes the dot product using expression [3; 4; 1]*[1, 4, 2]. Then, it evaluates the outer product using expression* $[3;\ 4;\ 1]*[1,\ 4,\ 2]$. *MATLAB function can also be used for vector multiplication as shown in the example.*

(b) Relational operation with vectors: *The two vectors can also be compared using the relational operator as mentioned in Table 3.5. For this operation, an element-wise comparison can be done. Moreover, the vector can also be compared with a scalar. To do this, it compares the scalar parameter with each element.*

Example: 4.6

Compute the output of the following expression

$$[5 \quad 2 \quad 6 \quad 1] >= [2 \quad 5 \quad 6 \quad 2]$$

Solution:

```
>> [5  2  6  1]>= [2  5  6  2]

ans =

    1 × 4 logical array

    1  0  1  0
```

(Continue using MATLAB function): *Compute the output of the following expression:*

$$[5 \quad 2 \quad 6 \quad 1] >= [2 \quad 5 \quad 6 \quad 2]$$

Solution:

```
>> ge( [5  2  6  1], [2  5  6  2])

ans =

    1 × 4 logical array

    1  0  1  0
```

(Comparison with scalar): *Compute the output of the following expression:*

$$[5 \quad 2 \quad 6 \quad 1] >= 2$$

Solution:

$>> ge([5 \quad 2 \quad 6 \quad 1], 2)$

$ans =$

1 × 4 *logical array*

1 1 1 0

(Comparison of row vector with column vector): *Compute the output of the following expression:*

$$1{:}4 <= [1 \quad 2]^T$$

Solution:

$>> le(1{:}4, [1; 2])$

$ans =$

2 × 4 *logical array*

1 0 0 0

1 1 0 0

Description of Example 4.6: *This illustrates the use of relational operators for vector comparison. Initially, in the expression* $[5 \quad 2 \quad 6 \quad 1] >= [2 \quad 5 \quad 6 \quad 2]$, *it compares element-wise and checks whether the condition is true or not? it displays '1' if it is true else '0'. Next, it uses MATLAB function 'ge()' to perform the aforementioned operation. This also compares the vector* $[5 \quad 2 \quad 6 \quad 1]$ *with a scalar value such that scalar value 'two' is compared with each element of vector* $[5 \quad 2 \quad 6 \quad 1]$. *At last, it compares a row vector* $1{:}4 = [1 \quad 2 \quad 3 \quad 4]$ *with a column vector* $[1 \quad 2]^T$ *and displays the output as* $\begin{bmatrix} 1\,0\,0\,0 \\ 1\,1\,0\,0 \end{bmatrix}$.

(c) Logical operation with vectors: *MATLAB allows the logical operation with the vector. It performs the element-wise operation using the logical operators (AND, OR NOT). Table 3.7 illustrates the basic logical operators.*

Example: 4.7

(AND operation without MATLAB function): *Consider* $v1 = [1 \quad 2 \quad 4 \quad 0]$ *and* $v2 = [2 \quad 0 \quad -1 \quad 2]$ *vectors. Compute the output of the following expression*

$$v1\ AND\ v2$$

Solution:

$>> v1 = [1 \quad 2 \quad 4 \quad 0];$

$>> v2 = [2 \quad 0 \quad -1 \quad 2];$

$>> v1 \,\&\, v2$

$ans =$

1×4 *logical array*

$[1 \quad 0 \quad 1 \quad 0]$

(OR operation Continue using MATLAB function): *Compute the output of the following expression using MATLAB function:*

$$v1\ OR\ v2$$

Solution:

$>> v1 = [1 \quad 2 \quad 4 \quad 0];$

$>> v2 = [2 \quad 0 \quad -1 \quad 2];$

$>> or(v1,\ v2)$

$ans =$

1×4 *logical array*

$[1 \quad 1 \quad 1 \quad 1]$

(NOT operation Continue using MATLAB function): *Compute the output of the following expression using MATLAB function:*

$$NOT\ v1$$

Solution:

$>> v1 = [1 \quad 2 \quad 4 \quad 0];$

$>> not(v1)$

$ans =$

1 × 4 *logical array*

$[0 \quad 0 \quad 0 \quad 1]$

Description of Example 4.7: *Initially, it creates* $v1 = [1 \quad 2 \quad 4 \quad 0]$, *and* $v2 = [2 \quad 0 \quad -1 \quad 2]$ *vectors. In AND operation without MATLAB function, It performs AND operation using '&' operator. As MATLAB allows its inbuilt logical operators, thus, it uses 'or()' command and 'not()' command to perform OR and NOT operations, respectively.*

4.2 Matrices

A matrix is a two-dimensional array often used for linear algebra. Consider a matrix $M_{i \times j}$, *where* i *denotes the number of rows and* j *denotes the number of columns.*

4.2.1 Matrices creation

A matrix is created by generating rows and columns. The row elements are isolated by putting either commas or space and column elements are generated by putting semicolons within the square bracket. Users can compute the number of row vectors and column vectors in a matrix A using $size(A)$ *command.*

SCAN ME
for more about matrix and array

Example: 4.8

Generate a matrix $M = \begin{bmatrix} 3 & 3 & 2 & 0 & 4 \\ 2 & 4 & 5 & 2 & 5 \\ 6 & 4 & 1 & 2 & 7 \end{bmatrix}$ *using MATLAB.*

Solution:

$>> M = [3 \quad 3 \quad 2 \quad 0 \quad 4; 2 \quad 4 \quad 5 \quad 2 \quad 5; 6 \quad 4 \quad 1 \quad 2 \quad 7]$

$M =$

```
3   3   2   0   4
2   4   5   2   5
6   4   1   2   7
```

(Computing the number of rows and columns): *Compute the number of rows and columns of a matrix M.*

Solution:

$>> sz = size(M);$

$sz =$

3 5

Description of Example 4.8: *Initially, it creates matrix M by separating row elements using space bar and column elements using semicolons. Then, it computes the number of rows and columns using $size(\cdot)$ the command. The number of rows and columns are 3 and 2, respectively. The significance of $size(\cdot)$ is realized when it creates another matrix or vector of the same size.*

Note:

- *A matrix whose number of rows is equal to the number of columns is called a square matrix. A square matrix S can be expressed as $S_{i \times i}$.*
- *A matrix with all the diagonal elements equal to one and the rest equal to zero, is called an identity matrix. The identity matrix is basically a particular case of the square matrix. In MATLAB, the user can create an identity matrix using $eye(\cdot)$ command.*
- *A non-square identity matrix can be created using $eye(m, n)$ command, where m and n is the number of rows and columns, respectively, and 1's are present only at the diagonal.*

Example: 4.9

Generate an identity matrix of size 3×3.

Solution:

$>> I = [1 \;\; 0 \;\; 0; 0 \;\; 1 \;\; 0; 0 \;\; 0 \;\; 1]$

$I =$

1 0 0

0 1 0

0 0 1

(Generate identity matrix using MATLAB function): *Create an identity matrix of size* 4×4 *using MATLAB function.*

Solution:

$>> I = eye(4)$

$$I = \begin{matrix} 1 & 0 & 0 & 0 \\ 0 & 1 & 0 & 0 \\ 0 & 0 & 1 & 0 \\ 0 & 0 & 0 & 1 \end{matrix}$$

(Generate non-square identity matrix): *Generate non-square identity matrix of size* 3×2.

Solution:

$>> I = eye(3, 2)$

$I =$

$$\begin{matrix} 1 & 0 \\ 0 & 1 \\ 0 & 0 \end{matrix}$$

(Generate identity matrix having same size of another matrix):

Compute the size of non-square matrix $M = \begin{bmatrix} 2 & 4 \\ 5 & 6 \\ 7 & 8 \end{bmatrix}$. *Also, create a non-square identity matrix of resultant size.*

Solution:

$>> M = [2 \quad 4; 5 \quad 6; 7 \quad 8];$

$>> sz = size(M)$

$sz =$

$$3 \quad 2$$

$>> I = eye(size(M), 'like,', M)$

$I =$

$$\begin{matrix} 1 & 0 \\ 0 & 1 \\ 0 & 0 \end{matrix}$$

Description of Example 4.9: *Initially, it creates an identity matrix of dimension* 3×3. *Identity matrices of dimensions* 4×4 *and* 3×2 *have been created using the command* $eye(4)$ *and* $eye(3, 2)$, *respectively. Also generate an identity matrix of the same size as the given matrix.*

In MATLAB, an array that contains all elements as ones or zeros can be created. It uses command $ones(\cdot)$ *to create an array which contains all elements as ones.* $zeros(\cdot)$ *command can be used to create an array containing all zeros.*

Example: 4.10

(Generate square matrix): *Generate a* 3×3 *square matrix whose all elements are one.*

Solution:

$>> O = ones(3)$

$O =$

$$\begin{matrix} 1 & 1 & 1 \\ 1 & 1 & 1 \\ 1 & 1 & 1 \end{matrix}$$

(Continue to generate non-square matrix): *Generate a* 3×2 *square matrix whose all elements are one.*

Solution:

$>> O = ones(3, 2)$

$O =$

$$\begin{matrix} 1 & 1 \\ 1 & 1 \\ 1 & 1 \end{matrix}$$

(Continue to generate a matrix consisting of all elements equal to one having same size to that of another matrix):

Generate a non-square matrix $M = \begin{bmatrix} 1 & 3 \\ 5 & 7 \\ 9 & 1 \end{bmatrix}$. *Also, create a matrix consists of all elements equal to one and having the same size as that of matrix M.*

Solution:

$>> M = [1 \;\; 3; 5 \;\; 7; 9 \;\; 1]$

$>> sz = size(M)$

$sz = 3 \quad 2$

$>> I = ones(size(M), 'like', M)$

$I =$

$$\begin{matrix} 1 & 1 \\ 1 & 1 \\ 1 & 1 \end{matrix}$$

Discussion of Example 4.10: *Initially, it creates a* 3×3 *matrix containing all elements equal to one using* $ones(3)$ *command. In Continue to generate a non-square matrix, it creates a non-square matrix of dimension* 3×2, *containing all ones. It creates a matrix which has the same size as the given matrix.*

Example: 4.11

(Generate square matrix): *Generate a 3×3 square matrix whose all elements are zeros.*

Solution:

```
>> z = zeros(3)
z =
   0  0  0
   0  0  0
   0  0  0
```

(Continue to generate non-square matrix): *Generate a 3×2 non-square matrix whose all elements are zeros.*

Solution:

```
>> O = zeros(3, 2)
z =
   0  0
   0  0
   0  0
```

(Generate a matrix consisting of all elements equal to zero and the size is equal to another matrix):

Generate a non-square matrix $M = \begin{bmatrix} 3 & 7 \\ 6 & 9 \\ 8 & 5 \end{bmatrix}$. *Also, create a matrix consisting of all elements equal to 1 and having the same size as that of matrix M.*

Solution:

```
>> M = [1  3; 5  7; 9  1]
>> sz = size(M)
sz = 3    2
>> z = zeros(size(M), 'like', M)
z = 0   0
    0   0
    0   0
```

Discussion of Example 4.11: *This generates a* 3×3 *matrix containing all elements equal to one using* $ones(3)$ *command. In Continue to generate non-square matrix, it forms a non-square matrix of dimension* 3×2 *containing all zeros. Finally, It creates a matrix which has the same size as the given matrix.*

4.2.2 Operation with matrices

(a) Arithmetic operation with matrices: *Arithmetic operation (addition, subtraction, etc.) with the matrices follows the same rule as the vectors. However, the multiplication rules follow the matrix algebra. Matrix multiplication can be done in two different ways.*

Scalar to matrix multiplication: *In this type of multiplication, it computes the product of a scalar with each element of the matrix.*

Example: 4.12

Multiply square matrix $M = \begin{bmatrix} 1 & 2 & 5 \\ 2 & 3 & 5 \\ 4 & 2 & 7 \end{bmatrix}$ *with scalar value* $\alpha = 3$.

Solution:

```
>> α = 3;
>> M = [1  2  5; 2  3  5; 4  2  7]
M =
     1  2  5
     2  3  5
     4  2  7
3 * M =
```

3 6 15

6 9 15

12 6 21

Matrix to matrix multiplication: *To understand the matrix multiplication, consider the two matrices,* A *and* B *which are having the dimension of* $i \times k$ *and* $k \times j$*, respectively. Multiplication of matrix* A *and matrix* B *gives the matrix* C*, where* $C = A \times B$*. The matrix* C *has the dimension* $i \times j$*. The dimension* k *and the dimensions* i, j *are known as inner and outer matrix dimensions, respectively. The matrix multiplication does not follow the commutative property, therefore,* $A \times B$ *is not always equal to* $B \times A$*.*

Example: 4.13

Consider the two matrices $A = \begin{bmatrix} 1 & 3 & 4 \\ 2 & 1 & 5 \\ 7 & 3 & 1 \end{bmatrix}$ *and* $B = \begin{bmatrix} 2 & 1 & 4 \\ 4 & 2 & 7 \\ 8 & 4 & 2 \end{bmatrix}$*. Compute the multiplication* $A \times B$ *.*

Solution:

```
>> A = [1  3  4; 2  1  5; 7  3  1]
A = 1  3  4
    2  1  5
    7  3  1
>> B = [2  1  4; 4  2  7; 8  2  2]
B = 2  1  4
    4  2  7
    8  4  2
>> C = A * B
C =
    46  23  33
    48  24  25
```

34 17 51

(Continue to compute $B \times A$): *Calculate the multiplication $B \times A$. Check whether matrix multiplication follows commutative property.*

Solution:

```
>> D = B * A

D =

    32   19   17

    57   35   33

    30   34   54
```

Matrix multiplication with identity matrix follows commutative property.

Solution:

```
>> A = [1  3  4; 2  1  5; 7  3  1]

A * I =

     1    3    4

     2    1    5

     7    3    1

I * A =

     1    3    4

     2    1    5

     7    3    1
```

Description of Example 4.13: *Initiated with assigning values to variables A and B. Then it computes the product $A * B$ assigned in variable C. Then, it evaluates matrix D which is equal to $B * A$. Here, we have seen that matrix C is not equal to matrix D. Hence, matrix multiplication does not follow the commutative property. Furthermore, multiplication with the* *identity matrix with any matrix follows the commutative property (when dimensions of matrix and identity matrix are satisfied), i.e.,* $A * I = I * A$.

(b) Relational operation with matrices: *Two matrices can be compared element-wise using the relational operators (for relational operators, see Table 2.5). It compares each element and the output '1' if the condition is true.*

Example: 4.14

Compute the output of the following expression

$$\begin{bmatrix} 4 & 2 & 5 \\ 3 & 9 & 6 \\ 8 & 1 & 4 \end{bmatrix} >= \begin{bmatrix} 3 & 4 & 8 \\ 8 & 7 & 3 \\ 3 & 5 & 4 \end{bmatrix}$$

Solution:

```
>> [4 2 5;3 9 6; 8 1 4]>= [3 4 8; 8 7 3; 3 5 4]

ans =

   3 × 3 logical array

   1  0  0

   0  1  1

   1  0  1
```

(Continue using MATLAB function): *Compute the output of the following expression using MATLAB function*

$$\begin{bmatrix} 4 & 2 & 5 \\ 3 & 9 & 6 \\ 8 & 1 & 4 \end{bmatrix} >= \begin{bmatrix} 3 & 4 & 8 \\ 8 & 7 & 3 \\ 3 & 5 & 4 \end{bmatrix}$$

Solution:

```
>> ge([4 2 5;3 9 6; 8 1 4], [3 4 8; 8 7 3; 3 5 4])

ans =

   3 × 3 logical array
```

1 0 0

0 1 1

1 0 1

(Continue comparison with scalar): *Compute the output of the following expression:*

$$\begin{bmatrix} 4 & 2 & 5 \\ 3 & 9 & 6 \\ 8 & 1 & 4 \end{bmatrix} >= 4$$

Solution:

$>> ge([4\ \ 2\ \ 5; 3\ \ 9\ \ 6;\ 8\ \ 1\ \ 4],\ 4)$

$ans =$

3 × 3 *logical array*

1 0 1

0 1 1

1 0 1

Description of Example 4.14: *Initially, it compares the expression using* $ge([4\ \ 2\ \ 5; 3\ 9\ 6;\ 8\ 1\ 4],\ [3\ 4\ \ 8;\ 8\ \ 7\ \ 3;\ 3\ \ 5\ \ 4]$ *command which scrutinizes element-wise. Next, it compares the same using the MATLAB function.*

(c) Logical operation with matrices: *Logical operations can also be performed with matrices. Element-wise operation is performed using the logical operators (see Table 3.7 for logical operators).*

Example: 4.15

(AND operation without MATLAB function): *Display the output of the following expression*

$$\begin{bmatrix} 2 & 0 & 1 \\ -2 & -1 & 0 \\ 0 & 0 & 2 \end{bmatrix} AND \begin{bmatrix} 1 & 1 & 0 \\ 3 & -1 & 0 \\ 2 & 0 & 4 \end{bmatrix}$$

Solution:

$>> v1 = [2 \quad 0 \quad 1; -2 \quad -1 \quad 0; 0 \quad 0 \quad 2];$

$>> v2 = [1 \quad 1 \quad 0; 3 \quad -1 \quad 0; 2 \quad 0 \quad 4];$

$>> v1 \,\&\, v2$

$ans =$

3 × 3 *logical array*

1 0 0

1 1 0

0 0 1

(OR operation using MATLAB function): *Display the output of the following*

$$\begin{bmatrix} 2 & 0 & 1 \\ -2 & -1 & 0 \\ 0 & 0 & 2 \end{bmatrix} OR \begin{bmatrix} 1 & 1 & 0 \\ 3 & -1 & 0 \\ 2 & 0 & 4 \end{bmatrix}$$

Solution:

$>> v1 = [2 \quad 0 \quad 1; -2 \quad -1 \quad 0; 0 \quad 0 \quad 2];$

$>> v2 = [1 \quad 1 \quad 0; 3 \quad -1 \quad 0; 2 \quad 0 \quad 4];$

$>> or(v1, v2)$

$ans =$

3 × 3 *logical array*

1 1 1

1 1 0

1 0 1

(NOT operation using MATLAB function): *Display the output of the following* *expression using MATLAB function:*

$$NOT\begin{bmatrix} 2 & 0 & 1 \\ -2 & -1 & 0 \\ 0 & 0 & 2 \end{bmatrix}$$

Solution:

$>> v1 = [2 \quad 0 \quad 1; -2 \quad -1 \quad 0; 0 \quad 0 \quad 2];$

$>> not(v1)$

$ans =$

3×3 *logical array*

$0 \quad 1 \quad 0$

$0 \quad 0 \quad 1$

$1 \quad 1 \quad 0$

Description of Example 4.15: *It initiates with assigning arrays* $[2 \quad 0 \quad 1; -2 \quad -1 \quad 0; 0 \quad 0 \quad 2]$ *and* $[1 \quad 1 \quad 0; 3 \quad -1 \quad 0; 2 \quad 0 \quad 4]$ *to the variables* $v1$ *and* $v2$*, respectively. Next, it performs the element-wise AND operation using '&' operator. Next, it performs the logical OR operation using MATLAB function* $or(\cdot)$*. It also accomplishes logical NOT operation of the variable* $v1$ *using the MATLAB function* $not(\cdot)$*.*

4.3 Sequence generation in MATLAB

Generationing a sequence of finite number of samples is widely used in applied mathematics, engineering science etc. Most of the periodic or aperiodic signals are expressed using a sinusoidal waveform where the time is varied in a specific pattern. It helps to produce these time-varying signals. A small array can be created manually. However, it becomes very difficult to create a sequence that consists of thousands or lakhs of samples, e.g. $[1\,2 \cdots 10000]$*. In MATLAB, a sequence of specific patterns can be generated using the colon. The formulation for generation of sequence is*

starting value : increment: end value

A user can form the sequence $[1\,2 \cdots 10000]$*, where 10000 is an arbitrary value, by considering initial value as 1 and final value as 10000 while considering incremental value is 1. The total number of samples are 10000.*

SCAN ME
for more about sequence

MATLAB has an inbuilt linspace command to generate the sequence. This command is helpful when the initial value, final value, and the total number of samples are known, whereas the incremental change is unknown. The expression for this command is $linspace(x, y, N)$, *where* x *and* y *are initial and final values, respectively, and* N *is the total number of samples.*

Example: 4.16

Generate a sequence whose initial value is 2, the final value is 10 and the total number of samples are 6.

Solution:

$>> z = linspace(2, 10, 6)$

$z = 2.0000 \quad 3.6000 \quad 5.2000 \quad 6.8000 \quad 8.4000 \quad 10.0000$

Generate a sinusoidal signal $x(t) = 2sin(4\pi\, t)$. *Select the time* t *such that initial value is 0, final value is 10 and total number of samples are 20.*

Solution:

$>> t = linspace(0, 20, 10)$

ans=

$0 \quad 2.2222 \quad 4.4444 \quad 6.6667 \quad 8.8889 \quad 11.1111 \quad 13.3333 \quad 15.5556 \quad 17.7778 \quad 20$

$>> x = 2 * sin(4 * \pi * t)$

$x = 0 \quad 0.6840 \quad -1.2856 \quad -1.9696 \quad 1.9696 \quad -1.7321 \quad 1.2856 \quad -0.6840 \quad 0$

Description of Example 4.16: *It generates a sinusoidal signal* x *of amplitude 2 unit and frequency of 2Hz. For the aforementioned information, the signal* x *at time instance* t *can be formulated as* $x(t) = Asin(2\pi ft)$. f *is the frequency of the signal, which indicates the total number of cycles completed in one second. If the time* t *is selected such that its initial value, final value, and total number of samples are defined. Then, it can compute the corresponding signal* $x(t)$.

Unit Summary

- *Vectors are represented either in terms of rows or columns*
- *Matrices consist rows and columns*

- *A row vector can be created by putting all elements in a square bracket and separated by using a space bar or commas*
- *Column vectors are obtained by putting all the elements in a square bracket where each element is separated by a semicolon*
- *Different operations can be performed on vectors and matrices*
- *Vectors can be added together, provided dimensions should be matched*
- *Vector addition and subtraction follow the distributive property*
- *Vector multiplication follows the element-wise multiplication*
- *A matrix can be created in MATLAB by separating row elements by space bar or commas and column elements by semicolons*
- *A matrix whose all the diagonal elements are equal to one and the rest are equal to zero is called an identity matrix*
- *MATLAB allows a generation of sequences that can be used for different applications.*

EXERCISES

Multiple Choice Questions

4.1 Which of the following is the correct way of creating a row vector?

(a) >> $var1 = [1; 5; 7; 4];$

(b) >> $var1 = [1, 5, 7, 4];$

(c) >> $var1 = [1: 5: 7: 4];$

(d) >> $var1 = [1. 5. 7. 4];$

4.2 Which of the following is the correct way of creating a column vector?

(a) >> $var1 = [1; 5; 7; 4];$

(b) >> $var1 = [1, 5, 7, 4];$

(c) >> $var1 = [1: 5: 7: 4];$

(d) >> $var1 = [1. 5. 7. 4];$

4.3 Compute the output of the MATLAB statement

>> 4 * [1, 4, 6, 3]

(a) [1, 4, 6, 12] *(b)* [4, 4, 6, 3] *(c)* [4 16 24 12] *(d) None of these*

4.4 Compute the output of the MATLAB statement

>> 4 * [1; 4; 6; 3]

(a) $[4\ \ 16\ \ 24\ \ 12]^T$ *(b)* $[4,\ 4,\ 6,\ 3]^T$ *(c)* $[1,\ 4,\ 6,\ 12]^T$ *(d) None of these*

4.5 Compute the output of the MATLAB statement

>> 4 * [1, 4, 6]

(a) $[4\ \ 16\ \ 24]^T$ *(b)* $[4,\ 4,\ 6]^T$ *(c)* [4 16 24] *(d) None of these*

4.6 Compute the output of the MATLAB statement

>> [2, 7, 3] ∗ [3; 2; 1]

(a) 23 *(b)* $[6,\ 14,\ 3]^T$ *(c)* [6, 14, 3] *(d) None of these*

4.7 Compute output of the following expression

>> [1 5 4; 6 0 2; 8 6 1] >= [1 2 0; 2 8 2; 1 6 8]

(a) $\begin{bmatrix} 1 & 1 & 0 \\ 1 & 0 & 1 \\ 0 & 1 & 0 \end{bmatrix}$ *(b)* $\begin{bmatrix} 1 & 1 & 1 \\ 1 & 1 & 1 \\ 0 & 1 & 1 \end{bmatrix}$ *(c)* $\begin{bmatrix} 0 & 1 & 1 \\ 1 & 1 & 1 \\ 1 & 0 & 0 \end{bmatrix}$ *(d)* $\begin{bmatrix} 1 & 1 & 1 \\ 1 & 0 & 1 \\ 1 & 1 & 0 \end{bmatrix}$

4.8 Compute output of the following expression

>> [8 5 4; 6 2 2; 4 3 1] >= [1 5 6; 1 6 4; 8 0 2]

(a) $\begin{bmatrix} 1 & 1 & 0 \\ 1 & 0 & 0 \\ 0 & 1 & 0 \end{bmatrix}$ *(b)* $\begin{bmatrix} 1 & 0 & 1 \\ 1 & 0 & 0 \\ 0 & 1 & 0 \end{bmatrix}$ *(c)* $\begin{bmatrix} 1 & 1 & 0 \\ 1 & 0 & 1 \\ 0 & 1 & 0 \end{bmatrix}$ *(d)* $\begin{bmatrix} 1 & 1 & 1 \\ 1 & 0 & 1 \\ 1 & 1 & 0 \end{bmatrix}$

4.9 Compute output of the following expression

>> *ge*([1 5 3; 8 6 0], [7 6 1; 3 9 4])

(a) $\begin{bmatrix} 0 & 0 & 1 \\ 1 & 0 & 0 \end{bmatrix}$ *(b)* $\begin{bmatrix} 1 & 0 & 0 \\ 0 & 0 & 1 \end{bmatrix}$ *(c)* $\begin{bmatrix} 0 & 0 & 1 \\ 1 & 1 & 0 \end{bmatrix}$ *(d)* $\begin{bmatrix} 1 & 0 & 1 \\ 1 & 0 & 0 \end{bmatrix}$

4.10 Compute output of the following expression

>> [9 5 8; 6 4 1] >= [5 7 1; 2 6 0]

(a) $\begin{bmatrix} 1 & 0 & 1 \\ 1 & 0 & 1 \end{bmatrix}$ *(b)* $\begin{bmatrix} 0 & 1 & 0 \\ 1 & 1 & 0 \end{bmatrix}$ *(c)* $\begin{bmatrix} 0 & 0 & 1 \\ 1 & 0 & 1 \end{bmatrix}$ *(d)* $\begin{bmatrix} 1 & 0 & 1 \\ 1 & 1 & 0 \end{bmatrix}$

4.11 Compute output of the following expression

>> [5 3 6; 9 2 1; 8 3 4] <= [5 1 6; 5 6 1; 8 7 6]

(a) $\begin{bmatrix} 0 & 1 & 1 \\ 0 & 1 & 0 \\ 1 & 1 & 0 \end{bmatrix}$ *(b)* $\begin{bmatrix} 1 & 0 & 1 \\ 0 & 1 & 1 \\ 1 & 1 & 1 \end{bmatrix}$ *(c)* $\begin{bmatrix} 0 & 1 & 1 \\ 0 & 1 & 0 \\ 1 & 1 & 0 \end{bmatrix}$ *(d)* $\begin{bmatrix} 1 & 1 & 0 \\ 1 & 0 & 0 \\ 0 & 1 & 0 \end{bmatrix}$

4.12 Compute output of the following expression

>> *le*([9 5 6; 1 8 0; 3 4 7], [8 1 4; 3 6 1; 7 9 6])

(a) $\begin{bmatrix} 1 & 0 & 0 \\ 1 & 1 & 1 \\ 1 & 0 & 0 \end{bmatrix}$ *(b)* $\begin{bmatrix} 1 & 0 & 1 \\ 0 & 1 & 1 \\ 1 & 1 & 1 \end{bmatrix}$ *(c)* $\begin{bmatrix} 0 & 1 & 0 \\ 1 & 0 & 0 \\ 0 & 0 & 0 \end{bmatrix}$ *(d)* $\begin{bmatrix} 0 & 0 & 0 \\ 1 & 0 & 1 \\ 1 & 1 & 0 \end{bmatrix}$

4.13 Compute output of the following expression

>> [6 5 1; 3 4 8] <= [3 7 1; 2 0 8]

(a) $\begin{bmatrix} 0 & 1 & 1 \\ 0 & 0 & 1 \end{bmatrix}$ *(b)* $\begin{bmatrix} 0 & 1 & 0 \\ 1 & 1 & 0 \end{bmatrix}$ *(c)* $\begin{bmatrix} 0 & 1 & 0 \\ 1 & 0 & 0 \end{bmatrix}$ *(d)* $\begin{bmatrix} 1 & 0 & 1 \\ 0 & 0 & 1 \end{bmatrix}$

4.14 Compute output of the following expression

$$>> le([9\ \ 4\ \ 3;\ 1\ \ 0\ \ 8],\ [9\ \ 7\ \ 1;\ 2\ \ 5\ \ 9])$$

(a) $\begin{bmatrix} 1 & 1 & 0 \\ 1 & 1 & 1 \end{bmatrix}$ (b) $\begin{bmatrix} 1 & 1 & 0 \\ 0 & 1 & 0 \end{bmatrix}$ (c) $\begin{bmatrix} 1 & 1 & 1 \\ 1 & 1 & 0 \end{bmatrix}$ (d) $\begin{bmatrix} 1 & 1 & 0 \\ 1 & 0 & 1 \end{bmatrix}$

4.15 Compute output of the following expression

$$>> [3\ \ 4\ \ 7;\ 1\ \ 8\ \ 9] > [1\ \ 6\ \ 8;\ 1\ \ 0\ \ 5]$$

(a) $\begin{bmatrix} 1 & 0 & 0 \\ 0 & 1 & 1 \end{bmatrix}$ (b) $\begin{bmatrix} 1 & 1 & 0 \\ 1 & 0 & 1 \end{bmatrix}$ (c) $\begin{bmatrix} 1 & 0 & 1 \\ 0 & 1 & 1 \end{bmatrix}$ (d) $\begin{bmatrix} 1 & 1 & 0 \\ 1 & 1 & 1 \end{bmatrix}$

4.16 Compute output of the following expression

$$>> gt([9\ \ 8\ \ 0;\ 4\ \ 3\ \ 6],\ [5\ \ 6\ \ 3;\ 1\ \ 2\ \ 4])$$

(a) $\begin{bmatrix} 1 & 1 & 0 \\ 1 & 1 & 1 \end{bmatrix}$ (b) $\begin{bmatrix} 1 & 0 & 0 \\ 0 & 1 & 1 \end{bmatrix}$ (c) $\begin{bmatrix} 1 & 0 & 0 \\ 1 & 1 & 1 \end{bmatrix}$ (d) $\begin{bmatrix} 1 & 0 & 1 \\ 0 & 1 & 1 \end{bmatrix}$

4.17 Compute output of the following expression

$$>> [3\ \ 6\ \ 3;\ 5\ \ 0\ \ 1] < [9\ \ 6\ \ 4;\ 7\ \ 8\ \ 3]$$

(a) $\begin{bmatrix} 1 & 0 & 0 \\ 0 & 1 & 1 \end{bmatrix}$ (b) $\begin{bmatrix} 1 & 0 & 1 \\ 1 & 1 & 1 \end{bmatrix}$ (c) $\begin{bmatrix} 1 & 1 & 0 \\ 0 & 1 & 1 \end{bmatrix}$ (d) $\begin{bmatrix} 1 & 0 & 0 \\ 1 & 1 & 1 \end{bmatrix}$

4.18 Compute output of the following expression

$$>> lt([1\ \ 9\ \ 4;\ 8\ \ 5\ \ 2],\ [1\ \ 3\ \ 8;\ 6\ \ 4\ \ 3])$$

(a) $\begin{bmatrix} 0 & 0 & 1 \\ 0 & 0 & 1 \end{bmatrix}$ (b) $\begin{bmatrix} 0 & 1 & 0 \\ 0 & 1 & 1 \end{bmatrix}$ (c) $\begin{bmatrix} 1 & 0 & 0 \\ 0 & 1 & 1 \end{bmatrix}$ (d) $\begin{bmatrix} 1 & 0 & 0 \\ 0 & 0 & 1 \end{bmatrix}$

4.19 Compute output of the following expression

>> eq([1 5 4; 8 6 2; 7 6 8], [1 2 0; 2 6 2; 1 6 8])

(a) $\begin{bmatrix} 1\ 0\ 0 \\ 0\ 1\ 1 \\ 0\ 1\ 1 \end{bmatrix}$ (b) $\begin{bmatrix} 1\ 0\ 0 \\ 0\ 1\ 0 \\ 0\ 1\ 1 \end{bmatrix}$ (c) $\begin{bmatrix} 1\ 0\ 0 \\ 0\ 1\ 1 \\ 1\ 1\ 1 \end{bmatrix}$ (d) $\begin{bmatrix} 1\ 1\ 0 \\ 0\ 1\ 1 \\ 0\ 1\ 1 \end{bmatrix}$

4.20 Compute output of the following expression

>> [6 3 4; 8 5 2] == [1 3 2; 8 7 2]

(a) $\begin{bmatrix} 1\ 0\ 0 \\ 1\ 0\ 1 \end{bmatrix}$ (b) $\begin{bmatrix} 1\ 0\ 1 \\ 0\ 1\ 0 \end{bmatrix}$ (c) $\begin{bmatrix} 0\ 1\ 1 \\ 1\ 0\ 0 \end{bmatrix}$ (d) $\begin{bmatrix} 0\ 1\ 0 \\ 1\ 0\ 1 \end{bmatrix}$

4.21 Compute output of the following expression

>> and([6 0 2; 1 8 3; 4 8 1], [5 2 7; 6 2 0; 8 3 4])

(a) $\begin{bmatrix} 1\ 0\ 1 \\ 1\ 1\ 0 \\ 1\ 1\ 1 \end{bmatrix}$ (b) $\begin{bmatrix} 1\ 0\ 1 \\ 1\ 0\ 0 \\ 1\ 1\ 1 \end{bmatrix}$ (c) $\begin{bmatrix} 1\ 0\ 1 \\ 1\ 1\ 0 \\ 1\ 1\ 1 \end{bmatrix}$ (d) $\begin{bmatrix} 1\ 1\ 0 \\ 1\ 1\ 0 \\ 1\ 0\ 1 \end{bmatrix}$

4.22 Compute output of the following expression

>> [1 4 6; 7 0 2] & [4 8 0; 1 9 2]

(a) $\begin{bmatrix} 1\ 1\ 0 \\ 1\ 0\ 1 \end{bmatrix}$ (b) $\begin{bmatrix} 1\ 1\ 1 \\ 1\ 0\ 1 \end{bmatrix}$ (c) $\begin{bmatrix} 1\ 1\ 1 \\ 1\ 1\ 0 \end{bmatrix}$ (d) $\begin{bmatrix} 1\ 1\ 1 \\ 1\ 1\ 1 \end{bmatrix}$

4.23 Compute output of the following expression

>> [9 0 7; 5 8 2; 4 0 0] | [5 0 7; 6 2 0; 9 3 0]

(a) $\begin{bmatrix} 1\ 0\ 1 \\ 1\ 1\ 1 \end{bmatrix}$ (b) $\begin{bmatrix} 1\ 1\ 1 \\ 1\ 1\ 1 \end{bmatrix}$ (c) $\begin{bmatrix} 1\ 0\ 1 \\ 1\ 1\ 0 \end{bmatrix}$ (d) $\begin{bmatrix} 1\ 0\ 1 \\ 1\ 1\ 1 \end{bmatrix}$

4.24 Compute output of the following expression

$$>> or([4\ 6\ 7;\ 6\ 0\ 2],\ [9\ 0\ 0;\ 3\ 0\ 8])$$

(a) $\begin{bmatrix} 1 & 1 & 0 \\ 1 & 0 & 1 \end{bmatrix}$ *(b)* $\begin{bmatrix} 1 & 1 & 0 \\ 1 & 1 & 1 \end{bmatrix}$ *(c)* $\begin{bmatrix} 1 & 1 & 1 \\ 1 & 1 & 0 \end{bmatrix}$ *(d)* $\begin{bmatrix} 1 & 1 & 1 \\ 1 & 0 & 1 \end{bmatrix}$

4.25 Compute output of the following expression

$$>> not([6\ 0\ 4;\ 2\ 1\ 1;\ 3\ 7\ 0])$$

(a) $\begin{bmatrix} 0 & 1 & 0 \\ 0 & 0 & 0 \\ 0 & 0 & 1 \end{bmatrix}$ *(b)* $\begin{bmatrix} 0 & 1 & 1 \\ 0 & 0 & 0 \\ 0 & 1 & 1 \end{bmatrix}$ *(c)* $\begin{bmatrix} 0 & 0 & 1 \\ 0 & 0 & 0 \\ 0 & 1 & 0 \end{bmatrix}$ *(d)* $\begin{bmatrix} 0 & 1 & 0 \\ 1 & 0 & 0 \\ 0 & 0 & 1 \end{bmatrix}$

4.26 Compute output of the following expression

$$>> \sim[4\ 6\ 2;\ 9\ 3\ 0]$$

(a) $\begin{bmatrix} 0 & 0 & 0 \\ 0 & 0 & 1 \end{bmatrix}$ *(b)* $\begin{bmatrix} 1 & 1 & 0 \\ 1 & 1 & 1 \end{bmatrix}$ *(c)* $\begin{bmatrix} 1 & 1 & 1 \\ 1 & 1 & 0 \end{bmatrix}$ *(d)* $\begin{bmatrix} 0 & 0 & 1 \\ 0 & 0 & 0 \end{bmatrix}$

Answers to Multiple Choice Questions
4.1 (b), 4.2 (a), 4.3 (c), 4.4 (a), 4.5 (c), 4.6 (a), 4.7 (d), 4.8 (a), 4.9 (a), 4.10 (a), 4.11 (b), 4.12 (d), 4.13 (a), 4.14 (a), 4.15 (a), 4.16 (a), 4.17 (b), 4.18 (a), 4.19 (a), 4.20 (d), 4.21 (c), 4.22 (a), 4.23 (a), 4.24 (d), 4.25 (a), 4.26 (a)

Short and Long Answer Type Questions

Category-I

4.1 What is the vector? Describe the methods to generate the row and column vectors.

4.2 Explain the operation on vectors using arithmetic, logical and relational operators with examples.

4.3 *How does a vector compare with another vector and a scalar? Explain with examples.*

4.4 *What are the matrices? Describe the methods to generate the matrices.*

4.5 *What is an identity matrix? How to generate a square and non-square identity matrices?*

4.6 *What is a zero matrix? How to generate a square and non-square zero matrix?*

4.7 *Describe the distributive property. Check the applicability of the distributive property for vectors with an example.*

4.8 *What is commutative property? Check the applicability of the commutative property for matrices with an example.*

4.9 *How to generate a sequence in MATLAB?*

4.10 *How does a matrix compare with another matrix and a scalar? Explain with examples.*

4.11 *Compare the inner and outer product of two vectors with an example.*

Category-II

4.12 *Generate a row vector* $[3\ \ 2\ \ 6\ \ 1]$. *Multiply it by a scalar value 4.*

4.13 *Generate a column vector* $[4\ \ 1\ \ 5\ \ 2]^T$. *Multiply it by a scalar value 3.*

4.14 *Add the two vectors* $[3\ \ 2\ \ 1\ \ 7]$ *and* $[4\ \ 1\ \ 3\ \ 8]$. *Check whether output of the addition can be added with the vector* $[2\ \ 5\ \ 1\ \ 9\ \ 4]$*?*

4.15 *Generate two vectors* $[1\ \ 3\ \ 3\ \ 7]$ *and* $[2\ \ 5\ \ 1\ \ 6]$. *Add the vectors and multiply the output vector with a constant value* $\alpha = 4$. *Check the applicability of the distributive property.*

4.16 *Compute the output of the following expression*

(a) $[4\ \ 6\ \ 2] \cdot [2\ \ 7\ \ 5]^T$

(b) $[3\ \ 4\ \ 1]^T \otimes [2\ \ 3\ \ 6]$

4.17 *Compute the output of the following expression:*

(a) $[4 \quad 4 \quad 2 \quad 1] <= 3$
(b) $[3 \quad 5 \quad 1 \quad 5] >= [3 \quad 4 \quad 2 \quad 6]$
(c) $1{:}5 <= [2 \quad 3]^T$
(d) $1{:}4 \sim = [2 \quad 1]^T$

4.18 Compute the output of the following expression
(a) $[2 \quad 3 \quad 4 \quad 0]\ AND \quad [1 \quad 0 \quad -1 \quad 0]$
(b) $[2 \quad 3 \quad 4 \quad 0]\ OR \quad [1 \quad 0 \quad -1 \quad 0]$
(c) $NOT[7 \quad 0 \quad 3 \quad 0]$

4.19 Create an identity matrix of the following size using the MATLAB function.
(a) 3×5
(b) 5×5

4.20 Generate a 4×3 square matrix whose all elements are one.
Generate a non-square matrix $M = \begin{bmatrix} 2 & 3 & 0 \\ 0 & 5 & 1 \end{bmatrix}$. Also, create a matrix consists of all elements equal to one and having the same size as that of matrix M.

4.21 Generate a 4×3 square matrix whose all elements are zeros.
Generate a non-square matrix $M = \begin{bmatrix} 2 & 3 & 0 \\ 0 & 5 & 1 \end{bmatrix}$. Also, create a matrix consists of all elements equal to one and having the same size as that of matrix M.

4.22 Consider the two matrices $A = \begin{bmatrix} 4 & 0 & 6 \\ 1 & 5 & 8 \\ 7 & 9 & 5 \end{bmatrix}$ $B = \begin{bmatrix} 4 & 1 & 3 \\ 1 & 2 & 2 \\ 6 & 4 & 0 \end{bmatrix}$, compute $A \times B$.
Calculate the multiplication $B \times A$. Check whether matrix multiplication follows commutative property?

4.23 Compute the output of the following expression

$$\begin{bmatrix} 1 & 3 & 5 \\ 8 & 6 & 3 \\ 7 & 0 & 4 \end{bmatrix} < \begin{bmatrix} 5 & 2 & 8 \\ 9 & 2 & 4 \\ 1 & 0 & 8 \end{bmatrix}$$

4.24 *Compute the output of the following expression*

$$\begin{bmatrix} 3 & 4 & 5 \\ 6 & 8 & 7 \\ 2 & 0 & 4 \end{bmatrix} AND \begin{bmatrix} 8 & 2 & 0 \\ 9 & 7 & 0 \\ 1 & 3 & 6 \end{bmatrix}$$

4.25 *Compute the output of the following expression*

$$\begin{bmatrix} 6 & 9 & 0 \\ 5 & 0 & 7 \end{bmatrix} OR \begin{bmatrix} 9 & 2 & 0 \\ 1 & 8 & 2 \end{bmatrix}$$

4.26 *Compute the output of the following expression*

$$\begin{bmatrix} 1 & 9 & 2 \\ 3 & 0 & 8 \end{bmatrix} == \begin{bmatrix} 1 & 7 & 2 \\ 8 & 0 & 4 \end{bmatrix}$$

4.27 *Compute the output of the following expression*

$$NOT \begin{bmatrix} 3 & 0 & 0 \\ 2 & 0 & 4 \end{bmatrix}$$

4.28 *Generate a sequence whose initial value is 5, final value is 20. Total number of samples is 10.*

4.29 *Generate a sinusoidal signal $x(t) = 4cos(6\pi t)$. Select the time t such that initial value is 0, final value is 20. The total number of samples are 30.*

PRACTICAL

Experiment 4.1: Experiment on vector operation

Aim

Design a half adder using MATLAB. Compute the sum and carry for the two vector inputs $A = [1 \;\; 4 \;\; 0 \;\; 1]$ and $B = [0 \;\; 1 \;\; 0 \;\; 1]$.

Apparatus

MATLAB

Theory

Half adder is a combinational circuit that adds two inputs (input can be a number, vector, etc.) and yields a sum and a carry as an output. The block diagram for half adder is as represented in Figure 4.1. The truth table for a half adder is as given in Table 4.1.

Figure 4.1: *Half adder*

Table 4.1: *Truth table for a half adder.*

Input A	Input B	Sum	Carry
1	1	0	1
1	0	1	0
0	1	1	0
0	0	0	0

The expressions for sum and carry are AB' + $A'B$ and AB, respectively.

MATLAB simulation

```
clear all
close all
clc
A = [1  4  0  1];
B = [0  1  0  1];
Sum = A & (~B) | (~A) & B
Carry = A & B
```

Results

Command Window
>>myprog

```
Sum =

    1×4 logical array

    1 0 0 0

Carry =

    1×4 logical array

    0 1 0 1
```

Conclusions

This experiment presents an application of vector operation as half adder. The two vectors are introduced as inputs to the half adder. The simulation results show the output in terms of sum and carry of the half adder.

Experiment 4.2: Experiment on matrix operation

Aim

Design an EX−OR gate using MATLAB. Perform the EX−OR operation for the two matrices $\begin{bmatrix} 1 & 0 & 3 \\ 0 & 1 & 0 \\ 2 & 1 & -1 \end{bmatrix}$ *and* $\begin{bmatrix} 0 & 1 & 2 \\ 1 & 2 & 4 \\ 0 & 0 & 1 \end{bmatrix}$.

Apparatus

MATLAB

Theory

EX-OR gate is the abbreviation of 'Exclusive OR gate'. It takes two or more inputs and gives one output as shown in Table 4.2. It gives the output as 'logic 1', when all the inputs are not at the same potential and 'logic 0' when all the inputs are at the same potential.

Table 4.2: *Truth table of Ex-OR gate.*

Input A	Input B	Output
1	1	0

1	0	1
0	1	1
0	0	0

The expression for EX-OR is $AB' + A'B$. It gives the output as logic '1' when both the inputs are at different potential and it gives the output as logic 0 when both the inputs are at same potential.

MATLAB simulation

```
clear all
close all
clc
A = [1  0  3; 0  1  0; 2  1  -1];
B = [0  1  2; 1  2  4; 0  0  1];
Output = A & (~B) | (~A) & B
```

Results

Command Window
>>myprog Output = 3×3 logical array 1 1 0 1 0 1 1 1 0

Conclusions

This experiment shows an application of matrix operation as EX-OR gate. The two matrices are introduced as inputs to the EX-OR gate. The simulation results show the output as 3×3 logical array.

Experiment 4.3: Generation of signal waveform

Aim

Generate a cosine waveform of amplitude two units and frequency 4Hz.

Apparatus

MATLAB

Theory

Mathematical formalism of cosine wave is

$s(t) = A_m cos(2\pi f t)$,

where A_m *and* f *denote the maximum amplitude and frequency of the wave, respectively.*

MATLAB simulation

```
clear all
close all
clc
t = 0:0.01:1
x=4*cos(8*pi*t)
figure
plot(t, x, 'k','LineWidth', 2)
xlabel('Time');
ylabel('Amplitude');
title('Cosine wave')
```

Results

Command Window
The plot of cosine wave is as shown in Figure 4.2. As 4 cycles are completed in 1 second , thus, its frequency is 4Hz. Peak to peak amplitude of the wave is 8 units.

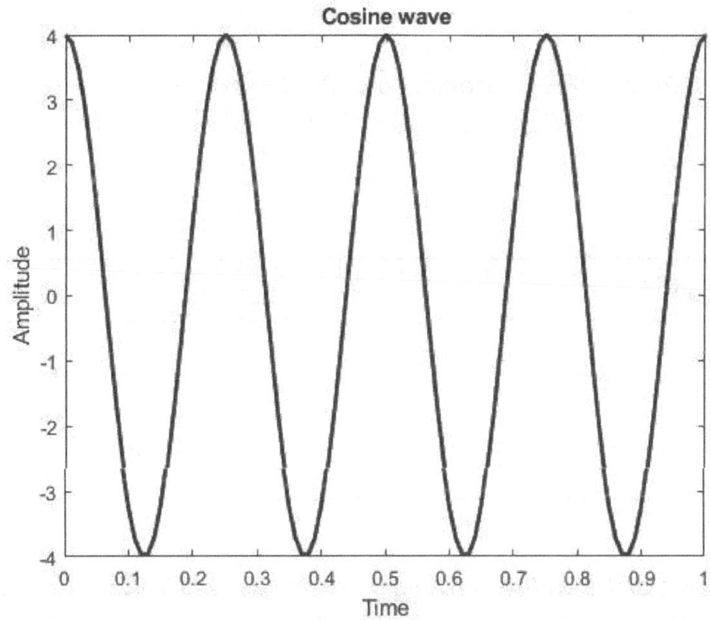

Figure 4.2: *Cosine wave*

Conclusions

This experiment demonstrates the cosine wave generation using MATLAB. Initially, it defines the time and mathematical formalism of the cosine wave. Then, it displays the plot of cosine waveform, so obtained.

Experiment 4.4: MATLAB program on convolution process

Aim

Compute the convolution of two vectors.

Apparatus

MATLAB

Theory

For the two vectors, x and y, the convolution shows the area between the x and y. Mathematically, convolution gives same results as polynomial multiplication. MATLAB uses conv(x, y) command to compute the convolution between two vector x and y.

MATLAB simulation

```
clear all
close all
clc
x = [2  4  1  2];          %Representation of 2x^3 + 4x^2 + x + 2
y = [2  0  3];             %Representation of 2x^2 + 3
z = conv(x, y)
```

Results

Command Window
>>myprog *z =* *4 8 8 16 3 6*

Conclusions

This experiment demonstrates the convolution of two vectors x=[2 4 1 2] and y=y = [2 0 3]. The output vector computed using the convolution is the multiplication of the two vectors i.e., z =[4 8 8 16 3 6].

5 MATLAB Scripts and Functions

UNIT SPECIFICS

This unit covers the following aspects:

- *MATLAB scripts*
- *Functions in MATLAB*
- *Different types of functions with applications*

This unit introduces MATLAB scripts and functions, which have a wide range of applications in different domains. It initiates with the creation of MATLAB scripts and the need for MATLAB functions. It also discusses the different types of functions which will help students with research and development. This includes a vast variety of solved examples that covers all types of MATLAB functions under different cases.

This unit contains a vast variety of questions, including multiple choice questions, and long and short answer-type questions. It follows the lower and higher order of Bloom's taxonomy. The lower order leads the students to understand, remember and apply for practical applications. Higher order skills improve students' creativity, analysis, and evaluation skills. This unit contains experiments which will help students to apply the content on practical applications. It has references and recommended readings through which students can explore more theoretical and practical aspects of the main content.

RATIONALE

This unit familiarizes students with MATLAB scripts and functions. Initially, it discusses the basics of MATLAB scripts and the procedure to save and execute a MATLAB program in the editor window. Next, it gives a brief introduction to MATLAB functions. MATLAB function programs consist of definition statements that include function keyword, inputs, and output arguments. This unit also covers the classification of MATLAB functions. It covers the local, nested, private, and anonymous functions. Apart from these, it also introduces the MATLAB handle and its type. This also contains a variety of examples to explain these functions.

PRE-REQUISITES

Basics of MATLAB environment

Operation with variables and matrices

Basic knowledge of linear algebra

Vectors and matrices in MATLAB

UNIT OUTCOMES

List of outcomes of this unit is as follows:

U5-O1: Describe MATLAB script

U5-O2: Functions in MATLAB

U5-O3: Different types of functions

Unit-5 Outcomes	EXPECTED MAPPING WITH COURSE OUTCOMES (1- Weak Correlation; 2- Medium correlation; 3- Strong Correlation)				
	CO-1	CO-2	CO-3	CO-4	CO-5
U5-O1	-	2	3	1	-
U5-O2	-	2	3	1	-
U5-O3	-	2	3	2	-

This unit covers MATLAB scripts and functions. Initially, it starts with the creation of MATLAB scripts. Next, it introduces MATLAB function and their different classification. This unit also discusses the examples of every possible formulation of MATLAB functions.

5.1 MATLAB scripts

A MATLAB script consists of a sequence of MATLAB commands or statements which are stored in m-file [1]. This employs an editor window to create a new script. In the editor file, the program statements are edited and saved. Following are the steps involved in creating the MATLAB script:

Step 1: *First create a new m-file by clicking on the new script file on the toolbar of MATLAB default environment as given below*

$Create\ new\ documents \rightarrow Script$ ( → )

New script can also be created by clicking $ctrl + N$.

Step 2: *The user must save the m-file to the desired location on the drive. To save the m-file, the user must click the save icon on the toolbar. The new script can also be saved by clicking* $ctrl + S$.

Step 3: *In the editor window, the user can write the program statement line, which includes the MATLAB functions, commands, expressions, etc.*

Note:

- *Script file has workspace along with its own current directory. Therefore, the variable names are carefully selected as there can be more than one variable of the same name. To get rid of this issue, users are advised to initiate the program with,* clc, $clear\ all$, *and* $close\ all$.
- *It uses the percent signs '%' to insert the non-executable text in MATLAB program statements.*

SCAN ME
for more about MATLAB scripts

Example: 5.1

Write a MATLAB script to evaluate the parameters of a cone of 2 unit radius and 5 unit height.
Solution:

```
clc
clear all
close all

% Mention the radius and height
r = 2;     %Radius
```

```
h = 5;      %Height

% Volume of the cone
Volume =  pi * r * r * h/3

% Lateral surface area of a cone
LSA = pi * r * (r^2 + h^2)^0.5

% Total surface area of a cone
TSA =  pi * r * (r+(r^2 + h^2)^0.5)
```

Command Window

```
Volume =
         20.9440
LSA =
         33.8360
TSA =
         46.4024
```

Description of Example 5.1: *Initially, it clears the command window, current directory using,* clc, clear all, *and* close d *commands. It assigns the radius and height of the cone to the variables 'r' and 'h,' respectively. This example displays the cone's volume, lateral surface area, and total surface area, which are assigned to the variables Volume, LSA, and TSA. This example also explains the use of the percent sign '%' to include non-executable text.*

5.2 Functions in MATLAB

Function is a series of commands in MATLAB to perform a given task. It consists of input and output arguments. The input arguments are accessible by the user after a specific command, which is known as 'function'. Output arguments contain the output after completion of the task. The syntax for defining a function is

$$function\,[z1, z2\,, \ldots, zM] = funname(x1,\, x2, \ldots xN) \tag{5.1}$$

where $x1, x2, \ldots xN$ are the N inputs and $z1, z2, \ldots, zM$ are the M outputs. $funname$ denotes the function name. Equation (5.1) is the definition statement and it must be the first line while defining a function [2].

5.2.1 Definition of function

In the editor window, the user can write the program statement line, which includes the word function followed by output, function name, and input.

SCAN ME
for more about functions

I. ***Function* keyword***: It is written in lowercase character.*

II. **Output:** *The output of the function is defined after the function keyword. The number of outputs can vary for the definition statement.*

   (a) *No output: MATLAB allows to omit the output when it is not required. A function with no output can be expressed as*

$$function = funname(x) \tag{5.2}$$

   (b) *One output: When there is one output in a definition statement, it must be written immediately after the function keyword. It is expressible as*

$$function\ output1 = funname(x) \tag{5.3}$$

   (c) *Multiple outputs: It also allows multiple outputs for a program statement. Multiple outputs are enclosed with square brackets as represented below*

$$function\ [output1,\ output2,\ output3] = funname(x) \tag{5.4}$$

III. **Function name:** *Following points should be noted while defining a function name:*

- *It must start with an alphabetic character.*
- *It can have numbers.*
- *It can also include the underscore.*
- *Special characters, e.g., #, $ are not allowed.*
- *Function name should match with the file name.*

IV. **Input:** *A statement definition can have one or multiple inputs separated by commas. Multiple inputs can be written within parentheses.*

$$function\,[output] = funname(x1,\ x2,\ \ldots\ xN) \tag{5.5}$$

If there is no input, then parentheses can be omitted.

Example: 5.2

(Valid function name): *Create a MATLAB function to print Hello India with its function name containing alphameric characters.*

Solution:

```
function PrintName1()
disp('Hello India')
```

```
end
```

Command Window

```
>> PrintName1
Hello India
```

(Continue for valid function name): *Create a MATLAB function to print Hello India with its function name as MyProg_2.*

Solution:

```
function MyProg_2()
disp('Hello India')
end
```

Command Window

```
>>MyProg_2
Hello India
```

(Continue for invalid function name): *Create a MATLAB function to print Hello India with its function name as MyProg#.*

Solution:

```
function MyProg#()
disp('Hello India')
end
```

Command Window

```
Error: Invalid Character
```

(Continue for invalid function name): *Create a MATLAB function to print Hello India with its function name as 2MyProg.*

Solution:

```
function 2MyProg()
```

```
disp('Hello India')
end
```

Command Window
Parse error: Invalid MATLAB syntax

Discussion of Example 5.2: *This example initially creates a function PrintName1 which displays 'Hello India'. MATLAB also allows the underscores in the function names as shown in the example. However, it does not allow the special characters like #, $, etc, and it gives an error. The function name should start with an alphabetic character otherwise, it displays Invalid MATLAB syntax.*

Example: 5.3

(No output): *Create a MATLAB function with no output.*
Solution:

```
function PrintName()
disp('Hello India')
end
```

Command Window
>> PrintName Hello India

(Continue with one output): *Create a MATLAB function to compute the average of numbers.*
Solution:

```
function Output1 = MyAverage(y)
Outout1 = sum(y(:))/numel(y);
end
```

Command Window
>> z = 1:4; >>Output = MyAverage(z) Output1 = 2.5000

(Continue with multiple output): *Create a MATLAB function to calculate mean, variance, and standard deviation of the data.*
Solution:

```
function [m, v, s] = MyProg(z)
n = length(z);
m = sum(z)/n;
v = (sum((z - m).^2 / n));
s = sqrt(sum((z - m).^2 / n));
end
```

Command Window:

```
DataValues = [10.32, 23.84, 86.93, 47.6, 34.17, 12.8];
[Avg, Var, SD] = MyProg(DataValues)
Avg =
    35.9433
Var =
    679.5538
SD =
    26.0683
```

Discussion on Example 5.3: *This example shows the function definition statement for different numbers of outputs.*

Example: 5.4

(No input): *Create a MATLAB function with no input.*
Solution:

```
function [x, y] = MyData()
x=[1.42, 5.23, 7.96, 3.14, 2.11];
y=[2.06, 3.08, 6.86, 4.87, 5.14];
```

```
end
```

Command Window

```
>> [x, y]=MyData()
x =
     1.4200    5.2300    7.9600    3.1400    2.1100
y =
     2.0600    3.0800    6.8600    4.8700    5.1400
```

(Continue for one input): *Create a MATLAB function to compute the area of a circle.*

Solution:

```
function [Area] = CircleArea(r)
Area=pi*r*r;
end
```

Command Window

```
Area = CircleArea(2)
Area =
        12.5664
```

(Continue for multiple input): *Create a MATLAB function to compute the area and perimeter of a rectangle.*
Solution:

```
function [Area, Perimeter] = MyProg(Length, Width)
Area=Length*Width;      %Area of the rectangle
Perimeter=2*(Length+Width); %Perimeter of the rectangle
end
```

Command Window

```
>> [Area, Perimeter] =MyProg(2, 5)
Area =
      10
Perimeter =
      14
```

Discussion of Example 5.4: *This example illustrates the function definition statement for different numbers of inputs. It starts without input where the function MyData displays the data assigned to variables x and y. Next, it uses one input to compute the area of a circle. The function definition statement also allows multiple inputs, as shown in the example.*

5.2.2 Function handle

A function handle denotes a function in MATLAB that moves a function to another function. It can be begun with a symbol @ followed by the name of the function [3]. Function handle express as

$$f = @MyProg$$

where $MyProg$ is the function. f denotes the function handle.

SCAN ME
for more about function handle

The function handles are further classified as

(a) *Named function handle includes the MATLAB functions and user-defined function keywords. It is created by using @ operator followed by the function name.*
(b) *Anonymous function handle denotes the single workable program statement which gives single output. It encloses the input within the parentheses after the @ operator, followed by a program statement. The major advantage of the anonymous function is that it allows multiple inputs and provides single output.*

Example: 5.5

(Named function handles): *Compute the zero of the cosine function if the initial value is 3.*
Solution:

```
>> f = @cos;        % function
z0 = 3;             % initial value
z = fzero(f, z0)
z =
    1.5708
```

(Continue for anonymous function handles) *Compute the output of the following* *integral*

$$\int_0^2 (z^2 + 2z + 1)dz$$

Solution:

```
function y = MyPoly(z)
y = z.^2 +2*z + 1;
end
```

Command Window

```
I = integral(@MyPoly, 0, 2)
I =
    8.6667
```

Discussion of Example 5.5: *This example illustrates the named and anonymous function handles. Initially, it evaluates the zero of the cosine function using named function handles for a given initial condition (z0=3). Here, cos and fzero are the MATLAB functions. It displays the output 1.5708 in radians (90 in degrees) when it executes z = fzero(f, z0). Next, it computes the output of the integral* $\int_0^2 (z^2 + 2z + 1)dz$ *using anonymous function handles. It starts with the definition statement function y = MyPoly(z), where the function keyword is followed by the output (y) and function name MyPoly and input (z). It displays the output 8.6667 when integral(@MyPoly, 0, 2) is executed in the command window.*

SCAN ME
for more about function types

5.3 Types of functions

A program statement can include numerous functions. It becomes complex to edit and read the program statements. Therefore, to make the MATLAB code readable, it is necessary to divide the program into compact tasks. On this basis, the function can be classified into the following categories:

(i) Local functions: *These are general methods to split the tasks. These functions are a sequence of program instructions accessible in the same file. The first function is known as the main function. The main function can be seen in other files. The other function in the same file is known as local functions. The order of calling the local function can vary, provided the main function remains the same. The local functions are also called as subfunctions [4].*

Example: 5.6

(Local functions): *Compute the volume and surface area of a sphere of radius 2 unit.*

Solution:

```
function [SurfaceArea, Volume] = myprogram(r)
SurfaceArea = myarea(r);
Volume = myvolume(r);
end

function A = myarea(r)                % myarea example of a local function.
A = 4*pi*r;
end

function V = myvolume(r)   % myvolume is example of a local function.
V=4/3*pi*r^3;
end
```

Command Window

```
>>[SurfaceArea, Volume] = myprogram(2)]
SurfaceArea=
            25.1327
Volume=
        33.5103
```

Description of Example 5.6: *This example computes the total surface area and volume of a sphere. Initially, it starts with the main function definition statement line, which includes 'SurfaceArea, Volume' as output arguments, 'myprogram' as the main function, and 'r' as input argument. Then it declares the two local functions i.e., myarea and myvolume. The local function myarea has the input and output as r and A. The local function myvolume has the input and output as r and V. It displays the output as 'SurfaceArea=25.1327, Volume=33.5103' when the program statement [SurfaceArea, Volume] = myprogram(2)] is executed in the command window.*

(ii) Nested functions: *These are accommodated inside a parent function. The variables defined in the parent function can be accessed and modified. This creates a handle in a* *parent function that includes mandatory data to execute the nested function [5]. Following are the requirements which should be fulfilled while using the nested function:*

- *All functions must have an end statement in the nested function program statements.*
- *Users cannot introduce a nested function within program control commands, e.g., switch/case, if/else, etc.*
- *Nested function can be called by either @ operator or by its name directly.*
- *Users must define all the variables in the nested function.*

Example: 5.7

(Nested functions): *Generate a MATLAB function to solve the following linear equation*

$$y = mx + c$$

Solution:

```
function L = LinearEquation(m,c)
L = @Line;
    function y = Line(x)
    y = m*x + c;
    end
end
```

Command Window

```
>> L=LinearEquation(2, 3);
>> x=2;
>> y=L(x)
y =
    7
```

Discussion of Example 5.7: *This example explains the nested function formulation to solve the linear equation. Initially, it declares function L = LinearEquation(m,c) as a definition statement, where L is the output, m and c are the inputs. LinearEquation is the parent function. Next, it defines the function Line using @ operator and output y = m*x + c. In the command window, it gives the output y=7 for x=2, when L=LinearEquation(2, 3) is executed.*

(iii) Private functions: *A private function is observable to a finite category of functions. These functions have applications where the user does not disclose the execution of the functions. These are saved in separate subfolders with specific names [6].*

Example: 5.8

(Private functions): *Compute the roots of the following quadratic equation using a private function.*

$$k_1 y^2 + k_2 y + k_3 = 0$$

Solution:

Editor Window 1

```
function D = Disc(k1, k2, k3)
D = sqrt( k2^2 - 4 * k1 * k3 );
end
```

Editor Window 2

```
function [y1, y2] = MyQuadratic(k1, k2, k3)
d = Disc(k1, k2, k3);
y1 = (- k2 + d) / (2 * k1);
y2 = (- k2 - d) / (2 * k1);
end
```

Command Window

```
>>[y1, y2] = MyQuadratic(2,4,3)
y1 =
        -1.0000 + 0.7071i
y2 =
        -1.0000 - 0.7071i
```

Description of Example 5.8: *This example illustrates the private function formulation to compute the roots of a quadratic equation. Initially, It declares the definition statement function D = Disc(k1, k2, k3) where Disc is the private function that computes the discriminant. This is to be saved in a separate subfolder in the working directory with the filename Disc.m. The output D is set as D = sqrt(k2^2 - 4 * k1 * k3), where k1, k2, k3 are the inputs to the definition statement. Next, create another editor window and define the function MyQuadratic, which has the output as two roots of the quadratic equation. In the* *command window, by assigning the value of the constant values as k1 = 2, k2 = 4, and k3 = 3, it displays roots of quadratic equation as y1= -1.0000 + 0.7071i, y2= -1.0000 - 0.7071i.*

(iv) Anonymous functions: *These are actually not present in program files but these are related to the variables which have function_handle data type. Anonymous functions can have many inputs and give a single output [7].*

Example: 5.9

(Anonymous functions): *Compute the output of the following expression for x = 1 using anonymous function formulation.*

$$\sqrt{x} + 2$$

Solution:

```
>> MyPoly1 = x.^0.5+2;
>> y = MyPoly1(1)
y =
    3.4142
```

(Continue to solve polynomial with coefficients): *Solve the expression* $y = m_1 z^3 + m_2 z^2 + m_3 z + m_4$ *for* y, *if coefficients* m_1, m_2, m_3, *and* m_4 *are 1, 2, 3 and 4, respectively. Assume* $z = 1$.

Solution:

```
m1 = 1;
m2 = 2;
m3 = 3;
m4 = 4;
MyPoly2 = @(z) m1 * z.^3 + m2 * z.^2 + m3 * z + m4;
```

Command Window

```
>> clear m1 m2  m3  m4
>> z = 1;
>> y = MyPoly2(z)
y =
    31.5000
```

(Continue for multiple anonymous functions): *Solve the following integral using multiple anonymous functions*

$$y = \int_0^2 (az + 1)dz$$

Solution:

```
y = @(a) (integral(@(z) (a*z + 1),0,2));
@(z) (a*z + 1);
integral(@(z) (a*z + 1),0,2);
y= @(a) (integral(@(z) (a*z + 1),0,2));
```

Command Window

```
>>y(2)
ans =
    6.0000
```

(Continue for anonymous functions with multiple inputs): *Solve the following expression*

$$z = (x + y)(x - y)$$

Solution:

```
MyPoly3 = @(x,y) (x - y )*(x+y);
z = MyPoly3(x,y);
```

Command Window

```
>> z =MyPoly3(2,1)
z =
    3
```

(Continue for anonymous functions arrays): *Store the functions* $(y^2 + 3)$, $(z^2 - 1)$, $(y + z)(y - z + 2)$ *using anonymous functions arrays and compute the value of the functions at* $y = 2, z = 4$.

Solution:

```
f = {@(y) (y.^2+3);
@(z) (z.^2-1);
@(y,z) (y+z)*(y-z+2)};
```

Command Window

```
>> y = 2;
>>z = 5;
>>f{1}(y)
>>f{2}(z)
>>f{3}(y,z)
ans =
      7
ans =
      24
ans =
      -1
```

Description of Example 5.9: *This example encapsulates the anonymous functions for different applications. Initially, it computes the value of polynomial* $\sqrt{x} + 2$ *using the anonymous function MyPoly1. Anonymous functions can also be used to solve the polynomials with multiple coefficients as shown in the example. It also allows multiple anonymous functions and multiple inputs. It can store several expressions simultaneously using the anonymous functions arrays as explained in the example.*

UNIT SUMMARY

- *MATLAB scripts consist of a series of commands or statements stored in an m-file. They are saved and edited in the editor window.*
- *Script file has workspace along with its own current directory.*
- *Function consists of input and output arguments.*
- *The syntax for defining a function is*

$$function\,[z1, z2\,, . . . , zM] = funcname(x1,\, x2,\, . . .\, xN)$$

- *A function can have zero or multiple input and output arguments depending on the task.*
- *Function handle helps to move a function to another function and it begins with a symbol @ followed by the name of the function.*
- *Function handle can be classified as*

(a) *Named function handles: It contains MATLAB functions and user-defined function keywords*
(b) *Anonymous function handles: It is a single workable program statement that gives single output*

- *The function can be of the following type*
  (a) *Local functions: Local functions are used to split the tasks into the subfunctions.*
  (b) *Nested functions: These are accommodated inside a parent function. The variables defined in the parent function can be edited and modified.*
  (c) *Private functions: These functions are saved in separate subfolders with specific names. They are useful when the user does not reveal the simulation of the functions.*
  (d) *Anonymous functions: Anonymous functions can have many inputs and give a single output. They are not present in program files but these are related to the variables which have function_handle data type.*

EXERCISES

Multiple Choice Questions

5.1 Which symbol is used to insert the non-executable text?

(a) & *(b) ~* *(c) %* *(d) @*

5.2 MATLAB scripts are edited in

(a) editor window *(b) command window* *(c) workspace* *(d) none of above*

5.3 In the following definition statement

$$function\ [z1, z2, \ldots, zM] = funcname(x1,\ x2,\ \ldots\ xN)$$

'$z1, z2, \ldots, zM$' *denote*

(a) outputs *(b) inputs* *(c) keywords* *(d) function name*

5.4 In the following definition statement

$$function\ [z1, z2, \ldots, zM] = funcname(x1,\ x2,\ \ldots\ xN)$$

'$x1, x2, \ldots, xM$' *denote*

(a) outputs *(b) inputs* *(c) keywords* *(d) function name*

5.5 Select the valid function name

(a) myfile$ *(b) myfile#* *(c) myfile_1* *(d) myfile@*

5.6 Which is not a valid function name

(a) Myprog *(b) Myprog_1* *(c) Myprog1* *(d) 1Myprog*

5.7 Which of the following program statement is correct to print New Delhi

(a)
```
function PrintName_1()
disp('New Delhi')
end
```

(b)
```
function 1PrintName()
disp('New Delhi')
end
```

(c)
```
function PrintName#()
disp('New Delhi')
end
```

(d)
```
function PrintName%()
disp('New Delhi')
end
```

5.8 Which of the following program statement shows a correct function with no output

(a)
```
function y= PrintName1()
disp('New Delhi')
end
```

(b)
```
function y=1PrintName()
disp('New Delhi')
end
```

(c)
```
function 1PrintName(x)
disp('New Delhi')
end
```

(d)
```
function PrintName(x)
disp('New Delhi')
end
```

5.9 Which of the following program statement shows a correct MATLAB function with one output

(a)
```
function y=myfun1(z1, z2)
y=z1 + z2;
```

(b)
```
function [y1, y2] = myfun(z1, z2)
y1=z1*ż2 - z1*z2;
```

```
end                                         y2=z1 - z2;
                                            end
```

(c)
```
function y= 1myfun(z1, z2)
y=z1+z2;
end
```

(d)
```
function [y1, y2] = myfun(z)
y1=z;
y2=z+4;
end
```

5.10 Which of the following is the correct way to begin a function handle

(a) $f\ =\ @MyFun$ (b) $f\ =\ \&MyFun$ (c) $f\ =\ \#MyFun$ (d) $f\ =\ \%MyFun$

5.11 Compute the output of the following in the command window

```
function y = MyPoly(z)
y = z + 1;
end
I = integral(@MyPoly, 0, 1)
```

(a) 2.0000 (b) 1.5000 (c) 3.0000 (d) None of these

5.12 Which of the following is the correct for solving linear equation $y\ =\ mx\ +\ c$

(a)
```
function L = MyEquation(m,c)
L = @Line;
    function y = Line(x)
    y = m*x + c;
    end
end
```

(b)
```
function L = MyEquation(m,c)
L = @Line;
    function y = L(x)
    y = m*x + c;
    end
end
```

(c)
```
function L = MyEquation(m,c)
L = @Line;
```

(a)
```
function L = MyEquation(m,c)
L = @Line;
```

```
    function y = L(x)
    y = m*x + c;
    end
end
```

```
    function y = Line(x)
    L= m*x + c;
    end
end
```

5.13 Which is not a type of MATLAB function

(a) Local	*(b) Nested*	*(c) Private*	*(d) Public*

Multiple Choice Questions Answers
5.1 (d), 5.2 (a), 5.3 (a), 5.4 (b), 5.5 (c), 5.6 (d), 5.7 (a), 5.8 (d), 5.9 (a), 5.10 (a), 5.11 (b), 5.12 (a), 5.13 (d)

Short and Long Answer Type Questions

Category-I

5.1 Define MATLAB script. How to create a MATLAB script?

5.2 What are MATLAB functions? What is the need for the MATLAB function?

5.3 Describe the MATLAB handles in brief.

5.4 Explain the different types of MATLAB function.

5.5 What are local functions? Explain with an example.

5.6 What are nested functions? Explain with an example.

5.7 Explain the private functions with an example.

5.8 Explain the anonymous functions with an example.

5.9 Consider the following definition statement for defining a function

$$function\ [z1, z2, \ldots, zM] = funcname(x1,\ x2,\ \ldots\ xN)$$

Describe the following condition with one example of each

(a) no input

(b) one input

(c) multiple input

5.10 Consider the following definition statement for defining a function

$$function\ [z1, z2, \ldots, zM] = funcname(x1,\ x2, \ldots\ xN)$$

Describe the following condition with one example of each

(a) no output

(b) one output

(c) multiple output

Category II

5.1 Write a MATLAB script to evaluate the perimeter of a rectangle of length 2 unit and width of 5 unit.

5.2 Create a MATLAB function to print New Delhi with its function name containing alphameric characters.

5.3 Create a MATLAB function to compute the average of the following

[2.12 4.34 3.97 5.11 7.32]

5.4 Create a MATLAB function to calculate the mean, variance and standard deviation of the following

[4.52 3.54 2.07 7.18 8.12 8.11 3.34]

5.5 Compute the zero of the sine function if the initial value is 1.5.

5.6 Compute the output of the following integral

$$\int_0^1 (z^3 + 2z^2 + z + 2)dz$$

5.7 Compute the area and circumference of a circle of radius 4 unit.

5.8 Generate a MATLAB function to solve the following linear equation for $x = 4$, $y = 5$.

$$y = mx + c$$

5.9 Compute the roots of the following quadratic equation for $k_1 = 3, k_2 = 4, k_3 = 5$ using a private function.

$$k_1 y^2 + k_2 y + k_3 = 0$$

5.10 Store the functions $(y^3 + y + 3)$, $(z^2 + 5)$, $(y^2 + z)(y + z - 5)$ using anonymous functions arrays and compute the value of the functions at $y = 5, z = 8$.

PRACTICAL

Experiment 5.1: Experiment on scripts and functions

Aim

Design a function to compute the area and perimeter of an equilateral triangle.

Apparatus

MATLAB

Theory

The equilateral triangle has equal sides. The perimeter of the equilateral triangle is $3 \times side$ and the area of an equilateral triangle is $\frac{3}{4} \times side^2$.

MATLAB simulation

```
clear all
close all
clc
function [Area, Perimeter] = myprog(side)
Area=((3^0.5)/4)*side^2;          %Area of the equilateral triangle
Perimeter=3*side;                 %Perimeter of the equilateral triangle
end
```

Results

Command Window
>> [Area, Perimeter] = myprog(5) Area = 10.8253 Perimeter = 15

Conclusions

This experiment presents a function that computes the area and perimeter of an equilateral triangle. Initially, it sets 'Area, Perimeter' as output and the side of the equilateral triangle as an input. Then it defines the mathematical formulation for area and perimeter of an equilateral triangle. Command window displays the results for perimeter and area when the side of the triangle is set as five.

References

[1] *'Programming and scripts', 2022 [Online]. Available: https://www.mathworks.com/help/matlab/learn_matlab/scripts.html [Accessed: September- 2022].*

[2] *'Function', 2022 [Online]. Available: https://www.mathworks.com/help/matlab/ref/function.html [Accessed: September- 2022].*

[3] *'Function handle', 2022 [Online]. Available: https://www.mathworks.com/help/matlab/ref/function_handle.html [Accessed: September- 2022].*

[4] *'Local function', 2022 [Online]. Available: https://www.mathworks.com/help/matlab/matlab_prog/local-functions.html [Accessed: September- 2022].*

[5] *'Nested function', 2022 [Online]. Available: https://www.mathworks.com/help/matlab/matlab_prog/nested-functions.html [Accessed: September- 2022].*

[6] *'Private function', 2022 [Online]. Available: https://www.mathworks.com/help/matlab/matlab_prog/private-functions.html [Accessed: September- 2022].*

[7] *'Anonymous function', 2022 [Online]. Available: https://www.mathworks.com/help/matlab/matlab_prog/anonymous-functions.html [Accessed: September- 2022].*

6 Branch Statements in MATLAB

UNIT SPECIFICS

This unit covers the following aspects:

- *if, if-else, if-elseif-else statements*
- *nested if-else statements and its application*
- *switch-case statements*
- *'is' function and its application*

This unit familiarizes the branch statements, which include if, if-else, nested if-else, and switch-case statements. It also covers the 'is" function in MATLAB. This initially introduces the if-else statements and the need for engineering science and mathematical science. Then it discusses the application of nested if-else statements and 'is' function in MATLAB.

This unit consists of various examples to improve the student's creative and logical skills. These will help the students to develop new ideas for different applications. It has a wide variety of unsolved multiple choice questions, and short and long answers type questions. This unit consists of experiments which will help students to apply the content on practical applications. This also contains the references and recommended readings through which students can explore more theoretical and practical aspects of the main content.

RATIONALE

This unit introduces branching statements in MATLAB. The branching statements include if, if-else, nested if-else and switch-case statements. The 'if expression' consists of relational operation-based expression, if this condition is satisfied, then the statement is executed. Nested if-else statements consist of 'if-else statements' and other if-else statements are within previous if-else statements. The switch-case statements contain 'case statements' to select the different choices available. These types of statements have several applications in engineering science, e.g., digital circuits, integrated circuits, etc. Apart from these, this unit also covers 'is function'. These functions have applications in detecting the state of the MATLAB entity. Each topic of the unit consists of examples to elaborate the content.

PRE-REQUISITES

Operation with variables and matrices

Vector and matrices in MATLAB

Functions in MATLAB

UNIT OUTCOMES

List of outcomes of this unit is as follows:

U6-O1: Describe about if, if-else statements

U6-O2: Explain nested if-else statements

U6-O3: Illustrate switch-case statements U6-

O4: Apply 'is function'

Unit-6 Outcomes	EXPECTED MAPPING WITH COURSE OUTCOMES (1- Weak Correlation; 2- Medium correlation; 3- Strong Correlation)				
	CO-1	CO-2	CO-3	CO-4	CO-5
U6-O1	-	1	2	3	-
U6-O2	-	1	2	3	-
U6-O3	-	1	2	3	-
U6-O4	-	1	2	3	-

6.1 Branching statement

MATLAB can perform several actions based on the situation. For performing these actions, it has decision-making commands, i.e., if, else-if, and switch statements [1]. These statements accomplish the program if the given conditions are satisfied.

6.1.1 if statement

MATLAB employs 'if statement' as a decision control command. if statement acts as a keyword in MATLAB, and it is always followed by the end keyword [1]. Following syntax is used for executing if statements:

SCAN ME
for more about if, elseif, else statements

```
if expression
statement (s)
end
```

(6.1)

In the above syntax for if statement, the expression is represented in terms of relational operator and checks for the applicability of the expression. If it is true, the statement is executed; otherwise, it will not be executed.

Example: 6.1

(if statement when the condition is true): *Check whether a number is greater than five. If the condition is true, then display 'Number is greater than five'.*

Solution:

```
>> N = 7;
>> if N >= 5
disp( 'Number is greater than five' )
end
```

Command Window

```
>>myfile
Number is greater than five
```

(if statement when condition is false): *Repeat the above when number is equal to four.*

Solution:

```
N = 4;
```

```
if N >= 5
disp( 'Number is greater than five' )
end
```

Description of Example 6.1: *This example illustrates the if statement for the two different conditions. Initially, it compares the variable N with the numeric value 5 for the condition 'greater than or equal to', and it displays the output as 'Number is greater than or equal to 5' as the condition is satisfied. The latter part of the example explains the if statement when the if condition is not satisfied, then It does not display the output for this case.*

MATLAB allows the comparison of the vectors and matrices also as the logical expression for equation (6.1). For this operation, it makes the element-wise comparison of the vectors or matrices. It will execute the program statements when the condition is fulfilled.

Example: 6.2

(if statement for vectors): *Check whether the sequence 3 : 7 is greater than or equal to three. Display 'Sequence is having the larger value' if the condition is satisfied.*

Solution:

```
if 3 : 7 >= 3
disp( 'Sequence is having larger value.' )
end
```

Command Window
>>myfile Sequence is having larger value.

(if statement for matrices): *Check whether the matrix* $\begin{bmatrix} 3 & 2 & 1 \\ 2 & 6 & 4 \\ 5 & 4 & 5 \end{bmatrix}$ *is equal to the identity matrix of size* 3×3.

Solution:

```
if [3 2 1; 2 6 4; 5 4 5] == [1 0 0; 0 1 0; 0 0 1]
disp('The matrices are equal.')
end
```

Description of Example 6.2: *This example explains the if statement for vectors and matrices. Initially, it creates a vector [3 4 5 6 7]. It compares the vector with numeric value three for 'greater than or equal to' condition. It displays the output as 'Sequence is having larger value' as the condition is satisfied. 'if statement' can also compare the matrices also on the element-wise basis as shown in the example.*

6.1.2 if-else statement

if-else statement in MATLAB checks the correctness of the expression. If the expression is true, it will execute the statement; otherwise, it will execute the false statement [1]. The syntax for if-else statements is

```
if expression
statement (s)
else                                                        (6.2)
statement (s)
end
```

The rational operator operates on the expression and checks the validity of the expression output.

Example: 6.3

(if-else statement): *Write a program to check whether the number is even or odd.*

Solution:

```
N = 6;                         % Enter the number
Expression = (-1)^N;           % Compute the expression
if Expression = = -1
    disp('N is odd')
else
    disp('N is even')
end
```

Command Window
>>myfile N is even.

A vehicle has traveled a total distance equal to 150 km in 1.2 hours. If the speed limit is 100km/h, find whether the speed is below or above the speed limit using if-else.

Solution:

```
D= 150;                        %Distance traveled in KMs
T = 1.2;                       % Total time taken in hours
S= D/T;                        % Speed of the vehicle
if S < 100
   disp( 'Vehicle speed is below the speed limit' )
else
   disp( 'Vehicle speed is above the speed limit' )
end
```

Command Window
>>myfile Vehicle speed is above the speed limit

Description of Example 6.3: *This example uses the if-else statement to check (i) whether the given number is even or odd, (ii) to compute the speed of a vehicle is below or above the speed limit. Initially, it computes the expression which is equal to (-1)^N, where N denotes the number. This displays the even number if (-1)^N is positive otherwise, it will display it as an odd number. MATLAB programming can also be used for computing and displaying vehicle speed, as shown in the example.*

6.1.3 elseif statement

The elseif statement is also decision control instructions. It computes the correctness and falsity of the expression and displays the corresponding results. The major difference between the if statement and the elseif statement is that the elseif also displays the result for the false statement. It first checks the authenticity of the statement, if it is false, then it computes the elseif statement [1]. The syntax used for executing elseif statements is:

```
if expression
    statement (s)
elseif expression
```

statement (s) (6.3)

else

statement (s)

end

In the above syntax for if statement, the expression is represented in terms of relational operator and checks for the applicability of the expression. If it is true, the statement is executed; otherwise, it will not be executed.

Example: 6.4

(if, elseif, else statement): *Check whether the mean of a sequence z=3:8 is within the range of four to six.*

Solution:

```
n = length(z);
Mean = sum(z) / n;
MinimumMean = 4;                    % Minimum mean value
MaximumMean = 6;                    % Maximum mean value
if (Mean > = MinimumMean) & & (Mean < = MaximumMean)
    disp( 'Mean is in specified limit' )
elseif (Mean > MaximumMean)
    disp( 'Mean is exceeding the specified limit' )
else
    disp( 'Mean is lower than specified limit' )
end
```

Command Window
>> myfile
Mean is in specified limit

Description of Example 6.4: *This example demonstrates the if, elseif, else statement to check the mean range. It initiates with defining all the variables. It then defines the if expression as '(Mean > = MinimumMean) & & (Mean < = MaximumMean)' and displays this* *as 'Mean is in specified limit'. Next, it also checks for the minimum and maximum limit of the mean, as shown in the example.*

6.1.4 Nested if-else statement

It contains another statement in them that is of the same type as the main statement. For example, when an if-else statement contains another if-else in it, it is said to be a nested if-else statement [1]. The syntax for nested if-else statement is

```
if expression
    if expression
    statement (s)
    elseif expression
    statement (s)
    else                                    (6.3)
     statement (s)
    end
else
    if expression
    statement (s)
    elseif expression
    statement (s)
    else
    statement (s)
    end
end
```

Example: 6.5

Write a program to demonstrate nested if-else statements.

Solution:

```
function [output] = MyProg(x, y)
```

```
if x>5
    if y<5
        output=2*x+3*y+5;
    else
        output=x-2*y+3;
    end
else
    if y>5
        output=x*y+y/x;
    else
        output=(3*x)/(2*y);
    end
end
end
```

Command Window

```
>> output= MyProg(5, 5)
output =
        1.5000
```

Description of Example 6.5: *This example demonstrates the nested if else statement. Firstly, it initiates a function with one output and two inputs (x, y). For the first if condition (x>5), it executes for (y>5) or (y<5). It gives the output 2*x+3*y+5 for y<5 and x-2*y+3 for y>5. In the second case, i.e., (x<5), it again checks for two conditions (y<5 and y>5) and gives the corresponding output.*

6.1.5 Switch case statement

SCAN ME
for more about 'switch case' statements

Switch case statement is useful when a user needs to accomplish one set of statements from many sets of statements. It uses 'case statements' to select the available choices. It considers the switch and case expressions as a scalar or a string [2]. The syntax for switch case statement is

switch expression 1

```
    case expression 2
        statements
    case expression 3
        statements
        ...
    otherwise
        statements
end
```

(6.4)

Initially, it computes the expression 1 and examines the given condition. It executes the corresponding statement if it matches the case expression. If the condition does not match with any of the cases, it will execute the otherwise statement. The main difference between if-else statements and switch-case statements is that if-else statements allow the vector expression, whereas switch-case statements do not.

Example: 6.6

Create a MATLAB program to simulate EX–OR gate using switch case statement.

Solution:

```
A = input( 'Enter the first input: ' );
B = input( 'Enter the second input: ' );
Output = (A & ( ~ B))|(( ~ A) & B);
switch Output
    case 1
        disp( 'Output is Logic 1' )
    case 0
        disp( 'Output is Logic 0' )
    otherwise
        disp( 'Other value' )
end
```

Command Window
Enter the first input: 1

```
Enter the second input: 1
Output is Logic 0
```

Description of Example 6.6: *This example illustrates the switch-case statement using EX-OR gate implementation. For the two inputs A and B, the EX-OR output is (A & (~ B)) |((~ A) & B). The switch expression contains this output. In the case expression, logic 0 and logic 1 are set. It gives the output as logic 0 for A=1, B=1 In the command window.*

6.2 is function in MATLAB

MATLAB uses the 'is' function to detect the state of the MATLAB entity. These functions have applications in several other statements, e.g., if-else statements, and switch-case statements, to check the correctness of the state of the MATLAB entity. Table 6.1 illustrates the 'is functions' in MATLAB [3].

SCAN ME
for more about 'is function'

Table 6.1: *is functions in MATLAB.*

'is' function	Description	Syntax	Example
isa	*It finds the object of the specified class.*	*x = isa(F, dataType)* *x = isa(F, typeCategory)*	*Check for single(2) is of single class:* *>>F = single(2);* *isa(F, 'single')* *ans = 1*
isappdata	*This function gets the information of a given application and data.*	*x = isappdata(obj,name)*	*Check the today's date :* *>>F = figure; D = date;* *setappdata(f,'todaysdate',d);* *>>isappdata(F,'todaysdate')* *ans=1*
isbanded	*isbanded function can be used to get the information of matrix bandwidth.*	*x =* *isbanded(A,lower,upper)*	*Check for the identity matrix bandwidth:* *>>I = eye(2);* *>>isbanded(I, 1, 1)* *ans = 1*
isbetween	*It denotes the array elements appearing in date and time gaps.*	*x=* *isbetween(t,lower,upper)*	*Find the time appearing between one to five for given lower and upper time:* *>>lower_t = seconds(2);* *>>upper_t=seconds(4);* *>>t = seconds(1:5);* *>>isbetween(t,lower_t,upper_t)*

			ans = 2sec 3sec 4sec
iscategorical	*iscategorica can check categorical array input.*	*x = iscategorical(F)*	*Check for the categorical array 'yellow' 'green' 'orange':* *>>F = categorical({'yellow' 'green' 'orange' });* *>>iscategorical(F)* *ans = 1*
iscategory	*It is used to find categorical array input.*	*x = scategory(F,catnames)*	*Check for the categorical array ["pen","pencil"; "rubber", "note"].* *>> F = categorical(["pen","pencil"; "rubber","notes"]);* *>>categories(F)* *statname = ["notes","shoes","table","pen"];* *>>iscategory(F, statname)* *ans = 1 0 0 1*
iscalendardurati on	*iscalendarduration can be used to check duration array input.*	*x = iscalendarduration(t)*	*Check duration array* *c1 = calyears(1:3);* *c2 = caldays(1:3); c = c1 + c2;* *iscalendarduration(c)* *ans = 1*
iscell	*It can be used to detect cell array input.*	*x = iscell(F)*	*Detect cell array {6, 7, 4; 4, rand(2, 1, 8), {1; 6; 8}}.* *>>F= {6, 7, 4; 4, rand(2, 1, 8),{1; 6; 8}};* *>> iscell(F)* *ans =1*
iscellstr	*It checks if the input is character vectors.*	*x = iscellstr(F)*	*Checks if the variable {'Delhi', 'Haryana', 'Mumbai'} is character vectors.* *>>C = {'Delhi', 'Haryana', 'Mumbai'};* *>> iscellstr(C)* *ans =1*
ischar	*It gets the information for input as a character array.*	*x = ischar(F)*	*Detect New Delhi as character array:* *>>c = 'New Delhi';* *>>ischar(c)* *ans =1*
iscolumn	*It checks for input as a column vector.*	*x = iscolumn(F)*	*Check for [1; 5; 8] as a column vector* *>> c = [1; 5; 8];* *>> iscolumn(c)* *ans =1*
iscom	*This gives the output as*	*x = iscom(F)*	*Detect COM object*

	logic 1 for COM object variables.		Excel.Application >>A = ctxserver('Excel.Application'); iscom(A) ans =1
isdatetime	It detects datetime array input.	x = isdatetime(t)	Detect date and time array: >>F = [datetime('now'); datetime('tomorrow'); datetime(2022,2,1)] F = 04-Aug-2022 15:17:20 05-Aug-2022 00:00:00 01-Feb-2022 00:00:00
isdiag	isdst checks diagonal matrix.	x = isdiag(F)	Check identity matrix for diagonal: >>I=eye(2) >> isdiag(I) ans = 1
isdst	This detects datetime happening in daylight time.	x = isdst(t)	Check for 2022,8,4 for Asia/Kolkata timezone happening in daylight time: DT = datetime(2022,8,4:11,'TimeZone ', 'Asia/Kolkata') isdst(DT) ans = 0 0 0 0 0 0 0 0

isduration	It checks for the duration array variable.	x = isduration(t)	Check for the duration array for dates 2022,08,16:17.
			>> time1 =
			datetime(2022,08,16:17);
			>>time2 =
			datetime(2022,08,20);
			>>dt = time2 - time1
			>> isduration(dt)
			ans = 1

isempty	It detects the empty array input.	x = isempty(F)	Check for empty array: >> F = zeros(0,1,1); isempty(F) ans=1
isenum	This checks if input is enumeration	x= isenum(F)	isenum function gives output as 1 if F is enumeration.
isequal	It detects equal arrays	x= isequal(X, Y)	>> I1=eye(2); >> I2=2.*eye(2)-eye(2) >> isequal(I1, I2) ans =1
isequaln	This checks for a numerically equal array.	x= isequaln(X, Y)	>> I1=ones(2); >> I2=2.*ones(2)-ones(2)

			>> isequaln(I1, I2) ans =1
isevent	It finds the COM object events.	x = isevent(c,eventname)	It gives output as 1 if an event perceived by COM object
isfield	This determines the structure array field variables.	x = isfield(F, field)	>>F.x = linspace(0,2*pi); >>F.y = cos(S.x); >>F.title = 'y = cos(x)'; >>isfield(F,'title') ans=1
isfile	isfile detects the input files.	x = isfile(fileName)	>>isfile(myfile1.txt) ans=0
isfinite	It checks for finite array elements.	x = isfinite(F)	>> F=1./[1 0 -1] >> isfinite(F) ans = 1 0 1
isfloat	isfloat are used to detect floating-point array inputs.	x = isfloat(F)	isfloat(10/3) ans =1
isfolder	isfolder detects the input as folder.	x = isfolder(folderName)	mkdir folder1; isfolder('folder1') ans=1
ishandle	It determines the justifiable graphics object handles	ishandle(F)	It gives the output as 1 when elements of F are graphics.
ishermitian	This detects the hermitian property of matrices.	x = ishermitian(F)	F =[2 2-i; 2+i 3]; ishermitian(F) ans =1
ishold	ishold detects the hold ON state.	x=ishold	ishold gives the current axes hold state.
isinf	Detect infinite elements of array	x = isinf(F)	>> F=1./[1 0 -1] >> isinf(F) ans = 0 1 0
isinteger	This find the integer array variable.	x = isinteger(F)	>>isinteger(int16(4)) ans=1
isinterface	This detects the COM interface.	x = isinterface(f)	It gives output as true for COM interface.
isjava	isjava determines Java object variable.	x = isjava(F)	Date1 = java.util.Date; isjava(Date1) ans =1
iskeyword	This checks for MATLAB	x = iskeyword(txt)	iskeyword('case')

	keyword.		*ans =1*
isletter	*It detects alphabetic letters.*	*x = isletter(F)*	*c = 'Delhi 16';* *>> isletter(c)* *ans = 1 1 1 1 1 0 0 0*
islogical	*islogical finds logical array in input.*	*x = islogical(F)*	*islogical(2==3)* *ans = 1*
ismac	*It checks for MATLAB version on the macOS platform.*	*x= ismac*	*It gives output if MATLAB version is for Apple macOS.*
ismatrix	*This detects the matrix as input.*	*x= ismatrix(F)*	*>> F=eye(2);* *>> ismatrix(F)* *ans =1*
ismember	*ismember checks the members of particular set*	*x = ismember(A,B)*	*ismember gives the output as true if data of A is based on B.*
ismethod	*This detects the object method input.*	*x = ismethod(obj,MethName)*	*It displays logical 1 when the method name is not hidden.*
ismissing	*It can detect table elements with misplaced values.*	*x = ismissing(F)*	*It displays logical 1 when input data is missing.*
isnan	*It finds the NaN array elements.*	*x = isnan(F)*	*>>isnan(0./[1 0 1])* *ans =* *0 1 0*
isnat	*It finds the NaT array elements.*	*x= isnat(F)*	*>>D = datetime(2022,[2 NaN 4 4], 5);* *>> isnat(D)* *ans =* *0 1 0 0*
isnumeric	*It detects numeric array variables.*	*x= isnumeric(F)*	*>>isnumeric(10)* *ans =1*
isobject	*This finds MATLAB object inputs.*	*x= isobject(F)*	*>>isobject(pi)* *ans =0*
isordinal	*This detects ordinal categorical array variables.*	*x= isordinal(F)*	*It returns logic 1 for ordinal categorical array.*
ispc	*This helps to determine it is executed on Windows platform for MATLAB*	*x=ispc*	*It gives output if the MATLAB version is for Microsoft Windows.*
isprime	*This function finds the prime elements.*	*x = isprime(F)*	*>> isprime([2 3 8 9 11])* *ans = 1 1 0 0 1*

isprop	*This checks object property.*	*x = isprop(obj,PropName)*	*It displays the logic 1 if the property name is object name.*
isprotected	*This function checks for protected categorical arrays.*	*x= isprotected(F)*	*It displays logic 1 if categories of F are preserved.*
isreal	*This determines real numbers in an array.*	*x = isreal(A)*	*>>isreal([1, 2, 6, 9])* *ans =1*
isregular	*This detects the regular timetable.*	*x= isregular(F)*	*>> isregular (seconds(1:3))* *ans=1*
isrow	*It checks for row vector input.*	*isrow(F)*	*>> isrow([2 6 7])* *ans =1*
isscalar	*This checks for scalar input.*	*x = isscalar(F)*	*>>F=eye(2);* *>>isscalar(F(1,2))* *ans=1*
issorted	*issorted function detects sorted order*	*x = issorted(F)*	*>> F=[4 7 10 15];* *>> issorted(F)* *ans = 1*
issortedrows	*This function determines the sorted rows.*	*x = issortedrows(F)*	*>> F = [1 4 8; 2 4 9; 3 0 6];* *>> issortedrows(F)* *ans = 1*
isspace	*This function finds the space in an array.*	*x = isspace(F)*	*c = 'Delhi 16';* *>> isspace(c)* *ans = 0 0 0 0 0 1 0 0*
issparse	*issparse function detects the sparse array.*	*x = issparse(F)*	*It displays logic 1 for sparse storage class.*
isstring	*This function checks for string arrays.*	*x = isstring(F)*	*>> S = ["Delhi","Haryana","Mumbai"];* *>> isstring(S)* *ans=1*
isStringScalar	*It checks for string array input consisting of a single element.*	*x = isStringScalar(F)*	*>> S="Delhi";* *>> isStringScalar(S)* *ans = 1*
isstrprop	*This checks for specified category input.*	*x= = isstrprop(str,category)*	*>> c = 'Delhi 16';* *>> isstrprop(c, 'alpha')* *ans = 1 1 1 1 1 0 0 0*
isstruct	*It detects the structure array input.*	*x = isstruct(F)*	*>> student.name = 'Rahul'; student.fee = 10000.00; student.marks = [67 65 83; 80 88 67.5; 69 71 78]; isstruct(student)* *ans = 1*

isstudent	*This finds if MATLAB is running in the student version.*	*x = isstudent*	*It displays logic 1 for student version MATLAB.*
issymmetric	*It checks for symmetricity of the matrix.*	*x = issymmetric(F)*	*>> F =[0 2-i; 2-i 0]; issymmetric(F) ans = 1*
istable	*This detects the input as a table.*	*x = istable(F)*	*It displays the logic 1 when F is a table.*
istabular	*This detects the input as a table or timetable.*	*x = istabular(F)*	*>>F = table([2;3.5],[1;3]); >>istabular(F) ans=1*
istall	*It checks for tall array input.*	*x = istall(F)*	*>>istall(tall(randn(100,2))) ans = 1*
istimetable	*This detects the timetable input.*	*x = istimetable(F)*	*>> Date = datetime(["2022-08-05";"2022-08-05"]); >>Temperature = [31.3;33.1]; >>Humidity = [68.9;71.2]; TimeTable = timetable(Date,Temperature,Humidity); istimetable(TimeTable) ans = 1*
istril	*This detects the lower triangular matrices.*	*x = istril(F)*	*>> F=[1 0; 1 1]; >> istril(F) ans = 1*
istriu	*This detects the upper triangular matrices.*	*x = istriu(F)*	*>> F=[1 1; 0 1]; >> istriu(F) ans = 1*
isundefined	*This helps to find out undefined elements.*	*x = isundefined(F)*	*It displays the output as logic 1 if the element of the categorical array of F is undefined.*
isunix	*This checks whether MATLAB is working on Linux.*	*x = isunix*	*It displays the output as logic 1 if the MATLAB version is for Linux.*
isvarname	*It checks for valid variable name*	*x = isvarname(v)*	*>> v = 'var_1'; isvarname(s) ans = 1*
isvector	*It detects the vector input.*	*x = isvector(F)*	*Check for the vector [1; 2; 5] >> F=[1; 2; 5]; >> isvector(F) ans =1*

isweekend	*This function finds if the given date is during the weekend.*	*x = isweekend(t)*	*Find the weekend date is during 2022,8,4:6.* *>> t = datetime(2022,8,4:6,'Format','ee e dd-MMM-yyyy')* *isweekend(t)* *ans = 0 0 1*

UNIT SUMMARY

- *'if statement' is a decision control command.*
- *The if-else statement evaluates the correctness and falsity of the expression and displays the corresponding results.*
- *The nested if-else statements contain another statement in it that is of the same type as the main statement.*
- *In switch-case statements, users accomplish one set of statements from many sets of statements.*
- *'is' function detects the state of the MATLAB entity.*

EXERCISES

Multiple Choice Questions

6.1 Following statement is included in branching statements

(a) iskeywords *(b) while* *(c) if-else* *(d) for*

6.2 Which of the following statement is not included in branching statements

(a) if-else *(b) nested if-else* *(c) switch-case* *(d) for*

6.3 In if statement, the expression is represented in terms of_________operator.

(a) relational *(b) addition* *(c) division* *(d) none of these*

6.4 Compute the output of the following statement

```
>> N = 7;
>> if N > 7
disp( 'Number is greater than 7' )
else
disp( 'Number is less than 7' )
end
```

(a) Number is greater than 7 *(b) Number is less than 7*

(c) Both (a) and (b) *(d) none of these*

6.5 Compute the output of the following statement

```
>> if N = 2:4<=4;
disp( 'Condition satisfied' )
else
disp( 'Condition not satisfied' )
end
```

(a) Condition satisfied *(b) Condition not satisfied*

(c) Both (a) and (b) *(d) none of these*

6.6 Compute the output of the following

```
D= 1000;          %Distance travelled in KMs
T = 10;           % Total time taken in hours
S= D/T;           % Speed of the vehicle
if 50 <=S && S <= 100
   disp( 'Vehicle speed is within the speed limit' )
elseif S > 100
```

```
        disp( 'Vehicle speed is above the speed limit' )
    else
        disp( 'Vehicle speed is below the speed limit' )
    end
```

(a) Vehicle speed is within the speed limit

(b) Vehicle speed is below the speed limit

(c) Vehicle speed is above the speed limit

(d) None of these

6.7 Compute the output of the following for x=3 and y=5

```
if x=5
   if y=5
       output=x+y;
   else
      output=x-y;
   end
else
   if y=5
       output=x/y;
   else
       output=x*y;
   end
end
end
```

(a) 0.6000 (b) 8 (c) -2 (d) 15

6.8 Compute the output of the following for A=1 and B=0

```
y = (A & B) | (( ~ A) & ( ~ B));
switch y
    case 1
        disp( 'y = 1' )
```

```
        case 0
            disp( 'y = 0' )
        otherwise
            disp( 'Other value' )
    end
```

(a) y = 1 (b) y = 0 (c) Other value (d) None of these

6.9 Compute the output of the following for A=1 and B=0

```
    y = (A & ( ~ B)) | (( ~ A) & B);
    switch y
        case 1
            disp( 'y =1' )
        case 0
            disp( 'y = 0' )
        otherwise
            disp( 'Other value' )
    end
```

(a) y = 1 (b) y = 0 (c) Other value (d) None of these

6.10 Which of the following is not a iskeyword

(a) elseif (b) end (c) for (d) and

6.11 Find the output of following program statement

```
>>S = ["Delhi",Chennai,"Mumbai"];
>> isstring(S)
```

(a) 1 (b) 0 (c) Both (a) and (b) (d) None of these

6.12 Find the output of following program statement

```
>>F=[1 0; 1  1];
>> istriu(F)
```

(a) 1 *(b) 0* *(c) Both (a) and (b)* *(d) None of these*

6.13 Find the output of following program statement

```
>>F=eye(2);
>>isscalar(F(2,2 ))
```

(a) 1 *(b) 0* *(c) Both (a) and (b)* *(d) None of these*

6.14 Find the output of following program statement

```
>>>>isobject(pi)
```

(a) 1 *(b) 0* *(c) Both (a) and (b)* *(d) None of these*

6.15 Find the output of following program statement

```
>>c = 'An apple';
>> isletter(c)
```

(a) 1 1 0 1 1 1 1 1 *(b) 0 1 0 1 1 1 1 0* *(c) 0 0 0 1 1 1 1 1* *(d) None of these*

6.16 Find the output of following program statement

```
>> F=ones(2);
ismatrix(F)
```

(a) 1 *(b) 0* *(c) Both (a) and (b)* *(d) None of these*

Multiple Choice Questions Answers
6.1 (c), 6.2 (d), 6.3 (a), 6.4 (b), 6.5 (a), 6.6 (a), 6.7 (a), 6.8 (b), 6.9 (a), 6.10 (d), 6.11 (d), 6.12 (b), 6.13 (a), 6.14 (b), 6.15 (a), 6.16 (a)

Short and Long Answer Type Questions

Category I

6.1 *What are the branching statements? Give a brief about the different types of branching statements.*

6.2 *Explain if statements with an example.*

6.3 *Explain if-else statements with an example.*

6.4 *What are nested if-else statements? Explain the significance of nested if-else statements with an example.*

6.5 *Explain the switch-case statement with an example.*

6.6 *What is 'is function'? Explain the following is functions with an example*

- *(a) iskeyword*
- *(b) iscolumn*
- *(c) isduration*
- *(d) isfinite*
- *(e) isinteger*

Category-II

6.7 *Check whether the sequence 6 :10 is less than or equal to 11. Display 'Sequence is having the smaller value' if the condition is satisfied.*

6.8 *Write a program to check whether the number is a multiple of three.*

6.9 *A vehicle has traveled the total distance equal to 750 km in 4 hours. If the speed limit is 80km/h, find whether the speed is below or above the speed limit using if-else.*

6.10 *Check whether the mean of a sequence z=6:12 is within the range of nine to ten.*

6.11 *Create a MATLAB program to simulate EX–NOR gate using switch case statement.*

6.12 *Check whether the dates 1 January 2023 to 5 January 2023 are during the weekend.*

6.13 *Create a MATLAB program to simulate half adder and full adder using switch case statements.*

6.14 *Check whether the matrix [5 7-4i; 7+4i 9] is a Hermitian matrix.*

6.15 *Check whether the matrix elements of 1 ./ [2 0 2 0]*

PRACTICAL

Experiment 6.1: Experiment on conditional branching

Aim

Design a thermometer that reads the temperature in Celsius and converts the results into Fahrenheit and displays the temperature level of the patient.

Apparatus

MATLAB

Theory

The temperature in Celsius can be converted to Fahrenheit using the following mathematical formalism

$$T_{Fahrenheit} = \frac{9}{5} \times T_{Celsius} + 32.$$

The average body temperature is between $97^{o}F$ *to* $99^{o}F$*, where F denotes the temperature units in Fahrenheit. A patient has a high fever if the temperature of the body is above* $100^{o}F$.

MATLAB simulation

```
clear all

close all

clc

T_Celcius = input('Enter the temperature in Celsius: ');

T_Farenheit = (9/5)*T_Celcius+32;

if (T_Farenheit>=97 && T_Farenheit<=99)
```

```
    disp('Normal body temperature')
elseif(T_Farenheit>99 && T_Farenheit<=100.4)
    disp('Moderate fever')
elseif(T_Farenheit>100.4)
    disp('High fever')
else
    disp('Temperature is below normal temperature')
end
```

Results

Command Window
>>myprog Enter the temperature in Celsius: 40 High fever

Conclusions

This experiment illustrates the application of conditional branching to design a thermometer. Initially, it takes the temperature in Celsius as an input and converts it to Fahrenheit. Next, it displays the patient's condition (whether the patient is normal. IIt also displays whether the patient has a high or moderate fever) according to the body temperature.

References

[1] 'if, elseif, else', 2022 [Online]. Available: https://www.mathworks.com/help/matlab/ref/if.html [Accessed: September-2022].

[2] 'switch, case, otherwise', 2022 [Online]. Available: https://www.mathworks.com/help/matlab/reThe legalf/switch.html [Accessed: September-2022].

[3] 'is functions', 2022 [Online]. Available: https://www.mathworks.com/help/matlab/ref/is.html [Accessed: September-2022].

7 Loop Statements in MATLAB

UNIT SPECIFICS

This unit covers the following aspects:

- *for loop*
- *nested for loop*
- *while loop*
- *time function and its application*

This unit introduces the iteration and time functions. Iteration includes for loop, nested for loop, and while loop. The time function consists of timeit, tic, and toc functions. The unit starts with the iteration function introduction and discusses several loop functions with their applications in engineering and mathematical science. It also covers time functions and its implementation on program statements.

The unit contains several solved examples from each topic to enhance the student's logical skills and develop a curiosity to apply in ongoing research applications. This unit consists of many unsolved multiple choice questions and short and long answers type questions. These will help the students to explore new ideas for different applications. The unit also consists of several references and recommended readings that help students explore more theoretical and practical aspects of the main content.

RATIONALE

This unit covers iteration functions, e.g., for loop, nested for loop, while loop, etc. for loop consists of a series of program statements that are repeated values of the given array.

In the case of a nested for loop, loop another for loop in it. The nested for loop has applications in iteration on 2-dimensional (2D) and 3-dimensional (3D) arrays. while loop executes the statement for indefinite times until the expression is false. Appended with these, this unit also covers the time functions. Time functions are used to measure the run time of program statements. It uses timeit and stopwatch timer (i.e., tic, toc) functions for this purpose. This unit comprises solved examples to explain the content for practical implementation.

PRE-REQUISITES

Basics of MATLAB environment

Operation with functions, matrices, and variables

Basic knowledge of branching statements

UNIT OUTCOMES

List of outcomes of this unit is as follows:

U7-O1: Describe for loop

U7-O2: Explain nested for loop

U7-O3: Illustrate while loop

U7-O4: Apply 'time function' for practical implementation

Unit-7 Outcomes	EXPECTED MAPPING WITH COURSE OUTCOMES (1- Weak Correlation; 2- Medium correlation; 3- Strong Correlation)				
	CO-1	CO-2	CO-3	CO-4	CO-5
U7-O1	-	2	1	3	-
U7-O2	-	2	-	3	-
U7-O3	-	2	-	3	-
U7-O4	-	2	-	3	-

7.1 Loop statements

The loop statements have applications where statements are repeated in a MATLAB script. In this case, the number of repetitions can be either known or unknown. If the number of repetitions is fixed, then the for loop is employed. On the other hand, while loop is used for the unknown number of repetitions. In this case, the number of repetitions is conditional, i.e., the three will be repetitions of the statements until the expression becomes false. Repeated program statements are known as looping statements.

7.1.1 for loop

SCAN ME
for more about 'for loop'

The for loop in MATLAB is a series of statements that are repeated for all values of the given array. The corresponding value of the variable with the current looping value is known as the looping variable. for loop is also called a definite loop as it has fixed initial and final values [1]. The syntax for for-loop is as follows

```
for index = values
    statements
end
```

Execution of the looping variable can take the following form:

Initial value-Final value – *The loop initiates with an initial index value and executes the statements; index value is incremented by one followed by statement execution. It repeats until it reaches the final value.*

Initial value-Step-Final value – *In this way, the loop starts with the initial value and executes the statements; the increment or decrement in this case is a step value on each iteration. Increment and decrement indices have positive and negative values, respectively.*

Value array: *It generates a column vector in the index form, and the number of iterations is equal to the number of columns of the array. Consider the array ValueArray, then the index for the initial iteration is ValueArray(:, 1). The ValueArray can have the form character, cell array data type, etc.*

Example: 7.1

Find the sum of array [1 2 3 4] using for loop.
Solution:

```
sum = 0;
F = [1, 2, 3, 4];
for k = 1 : length (F)
sum = sum + F(k)
```

```
end
```

Command Window

```
>> myprog
sum =
      10
```

(Continue to compute the sum of the cube): *Compute the sum of the cube of all numbers from 1 to 5.*
Solution:

```
sum = 0;
for k = 1:5
    k = k^3;
    sum = sum + k
end
```

Command Window

```
>> myprog
sum =
      225
```

*(***Continue to compute the sum of the random array***): Calculate the sum of the array [1:4, 7] using for loop.*
Solution:

```
m=0;
F=[1:4, 7];
for k = 1 : length (F)
    m=m + F(k)
end
```

Command Window

```
>>myprog
```

```
m =

    17
```

Description of Example 7.1: *This example illustrates the summation of elements of an array. It initializes with the summation value as zero and defines the array to the variable F. It begins the for loop with the expression 'k = 1 : length (F)', where the loop starts at k=1 and goes up to a length of array F. Then, it computes the sum using 'sum=sum + F(k)'. For k=1, the sum is equal to 1. Similarly, for k=2, the sum is equal to 3. The sum is equal to 10 for k=4. The for loop can be used to compute the sum of the cube of the series. The users can also use this loop for computing the sum of all array elements, as shown in the example.*

7.1.2 Nested for loop

When a for loop contains another for loop, it is said to be a nested for loop statement. The nested for loop has the application in iteration required in a 2-dimensional array (2D). It can also be used for 3-dimensional (3D) arrays. For 3D applications, the nested for loop contains another nested for loop.

Example: 7.2

Find the prime number from 2 to 20 using a nested for loop.
Solution:

```
for p = 2:20
  for q = 2:20
    if(~mod(p,q))
      break;
    end
  end
  if(n > (p/q))
     fprintf('%d\n', p);
  end
end
```

Command Window

```
>>myprog
2
```

```
3
5
7
11
13
17
19
```

(Continue to calculate sum of all elements of matrix):

Compute the sum of all the elements of the matrix $\begin{bmatrix} 3 & 2 & 4 \\ 8 & 1 & 7 \\ 6 & 2 & 1 \end{bmatrix}$ *using a nested for loop.*

Solution:

```
F=[3  2  4; 8  1  7; 6  2  1];
sum = 0;
for m = 1:3
   for n=1:3
      sum = sum + F(m, n)
   end
end
```

Command Window

```
>> myprog
sum =
       34
```

Description of Example 7.2: *This example explains the application of nested for loop. Nested for loop can be used to find the prime numbers, as shown in the example. The break keyword stops the loop for the next value of m or n if the condition ~mod(m,n) is satisfied. Nested for loop can also be used to add all elements of matrices, as shown in the example.*

7.1.3 while loop

The while loop in MATLAB executes the statement for indefinite times until the expression is false. while loop is also called an indefinite loop as statements are computed repeatedly until the expression is false [2]. The syntax for a while loop is

SCAN ME
for more about 'while loop'

```
while expression
    statements
end
```

The while loop first computes the expressions, then statements are executed. When the output of the expression is not empty or has elements in the form of numerical or logical values, then it is said to be true. For the true expression, it computes the statements and repeats them until the expression is false.

Example: 7.3

How many times can 81 be divided by 3 such that the result is less than unity?

Solution:

```
m = 0;
M = 81;
while M >= 1
    M = M/3;
    m=m+1
end
```

Command Window

```
>> myprog
m =
    5
```

Description of Example 7.3: *This example illustrates the while loop for computing the number of divisions possible. Initially. it initiates with initializing number (M) and divisor. Next, it applies the condition M >= 1, if this condition is satisfied, then it computes M = M/3; otherwise, it will stop.*

7.2 Timing functions

MATLAB uses timeit, and stopwatch timer (i.e., tic, toc) functions to measure program statements' run time. It uses tic and toc for execution time estimation of a small part of the program, whereas MATLAB profiler is used for supplementary information of the execution of the program, e.g., the execution time of each code line.

SCAN ME
for more about timing function

7.2.1 timeit function

Users can employ timeit function to compute the time needed to execute a function. It recalls a function several times and gives the median as output. The syntax for timeit function is

t = timeit(f)

t = timeit(f,NumberofOutputs)

where t is the measured time (in seconds) using timeit function. f represents a function described by the function handle. MATLAB allows recalling the function f with requisitioned number of outputs. It uses timeit(f,NumberofOutputs) for this purpose. The value of NumberofOutputs is unity by default.

7.2.2 tic and toc function

The tic function in MATLAB can be used to compute the elapsed time. The toc function follows this function. The tic function and toc function measure initial time and traced time, respectively, to give the total elapsed time as output. The syntax for tic and toc function is

tic

program statement

toc

It initiates with setting the initial time after the application of the tic function. This will store the current time. Then, the program statements are executed. Finally, it records the total time elapsed using the toc function.

Note:

- *The two or more successive calls lead to overwriting the previous stored initial time.*
- *Initial time measured using tic function remains unaffected using clear function.*
- *If the program statement run time is faster than 0.1 second, then it is preferable to compute the average for a single run.*

Example: 7.4

Write a program to perform the arithmetic operation with sinusoidal signals and compute the execution time using timeit function.

Solution:

```
>> t=0 : .01 : 1;
>> x = 2.5*sin(4*pi*t);
>> y = 5.0*cos(8*pi*t);
>> f = @() sum(x.*y, 1);
>>timeit(f)
ans =
      4.7846e-06
```

(Continue to use tic and toc functions): *Consider Example 7.2, compute the total elapsed time using tic and toc function.*

Solution:

```
tic
F=[3  2  4; 8  1  7; 6  2  1];
sum = 0;
for m = 1:3
   for n=1:3
      sum = sum + F(m, n);
   end
end
toc
```

Command Window

```
>>myprog
Elapsed time is 0.072386 seconds.
```

(Continue to use a combination of tic, toc functions): *Consider Example 7.4, compute the overall time needed for an element by element matrix product using a combination of tic and toc functions.*

Solution:

```
t_start= tic;
m = 10;
N = zeros(1,m);
for j = 1:m
   t = 0 : 0 .01 : 1;
   x =5* sin(4*pi*t);
   y =25* cos(8*pi*t);
   f = @() sum(x.*y, 1);
   T(j) = toc;
end
N_total = sum(N)
```

Command Window

```
>>myprog
T_total =
            9.17023e+06
```

Description of Example 7.4: *This example illustrates the application of timeit function for computing the time required for performing the arithmetic operation of two sinusoidal signal. Initially, it defines the time period of the signal and two sinusoidal signals. It performs the arithmetic operation for two sinusoidal signals. The execution time for the program statements is computed using the timeit function. The tic and toc functions can also be used for measuring the execution time of the program, as shown in the example. It begins with tic function, followed by a program statement. The toc function records the total time elapsed by the program. A combination of tic, toc functions can also be used for the element-by-element matrix product, as shown in the example.*

7.3 Profiling to enhance performance

Profiling is a method to check the execution time of each function. This helps in improving performance. The users can also profile the program statements as a debugging mechanism. Profiling can also be used to locate the error in the program statements so that it can be corrected. Following are the steps involved in profiling the code:

SCAN ME
for more about Profiling

1) *It initiates by typing 'profile on' in the command window.*
2) *After this, the execution of program statements takes place.*

3) *After program statement execution, the user can type profile off.*
4) *profile viewer can be used to check the profile summary.*

Example: 7.5

Profile the MATLAB code for Example 7.4. Also illustrate the profile summary.
Solution:

```
>> profile on
>> t = 0 : .01 : 10;
>> x = sin(4*pi*t);
>>y = sin(8*pi*t);
>>f = @() sum(x.*y, 1);
>> profile off
>> profile viewer
```

Description of Example 7.5: *This example demonstrates the application of profiling to improve the performance of the MATLAB code. This begins with 'turning on' the profile by typing 'profile on' followed by program statements. After executing the program statements, the profiling is disabled using 'profile off'. The profile summary can be displayed using profile viewer command statement. Figure 7.1 illustrates the profile summary of the example.*

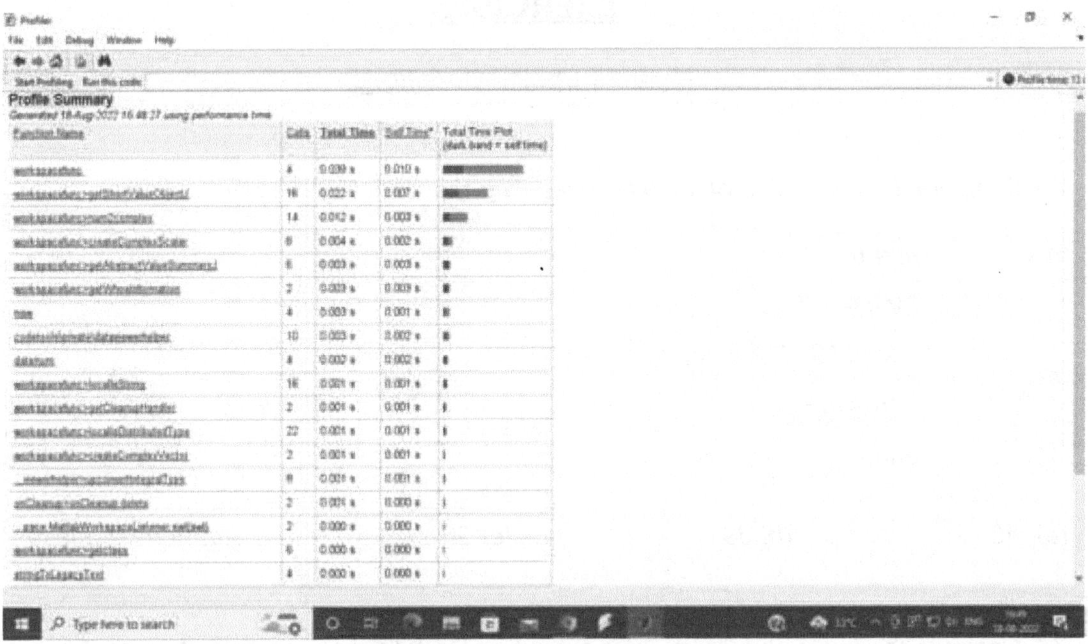

Figure 7.1: *Profile summary*

UNIT SUMMARY

- *The for loop in MATLAB is a sequence of statements that are repeated for the specified array.*
- *The variable with the current looping value is known as the looping variable.*
- *If a for loop contains another for loop, then this is said to be a nested for loop statement. One nested for loop can contain another nested for loop.*
- *while loop executes the statement for indefinite times until the expression is false. As loops are executed for indefinite times, thus these are also known as an indefinite loop.*
- *Time functions measure the execution time of a program statement. It uses the following function for this*
    - *timeit*
    - *tic and toc functions*
- *Profiling is used to check the execution time, which helps improve the program statement's performance and reduces the possibility of error.*

EXERCISES

Multiple Choice Questions

7.1 Compute the final value of 'm' after executing the following program statement

```
m = 0;
for k = 1:3
  k = k^3+2;
  m = m + k
end
```

(a) 42 *(b) 39* *(c) 36* *(d) none of these*

7.2 Compute the final value of 'm' after executing the following program statement

```
m = 0;
for k = 1:3
  k = k^2+2*k;
  m = m + k
end
```

(a) 30 (b) 12 (c) 16 (d) 26

7.3 Compute the final value of 'm' after executing the following program statement

```
m=0;
F=[1, 4, 3]
for k = 1 : length (F)
   m=m + k*F(k)
end
```

(a) 8 (b) 18 (c) 10 (d) none of these

7.4 What is the value of 's' after executing the following program statement

```
F=[1  3  1; 2  5  9; 5  3  2];
s = 0;
for m = 1:3
   for n=1:3
        s = s + F(m, n)
   end
end
```

(a) 31 (b) 21 (c) 18 (d) none of these

7.5 Compute the final value of 's' after executing the following program statement

```
F=eye(3);
s = 0;
for p = 1:3
   for q=1:3
        s = p*s + q*F(p, q)
   end
end
```

(a) 320 *(b)127* *(c) 327* *(d) none of these*

7.6 Compute the final value of 's' after executing the following program statement

```
F=[1  3  1; 2  5  9;  5  3  2];
s = 0;
for p = 1:3
   for q=1:3
        s = s + F(p, q)
   end
end
```

(a) 31 *(b) 21* *(c) 18* *(d) none of these*

7.7 Compute the final value of 'm' after executing the following program statement

```
m = 0;
M = 27;
while M >= 1
    M = M/3;
    m=m+1
end
```

(a) 5 *(b) 4* *(c) 3* *(d) none of these*

7.8 Incremental value for 'for loop' is

(a) 1 *(b) 2* *(c) not defined* *(d) none of these*

7.9 Which loop is used when number of repetitions are fixed

(a) while (b) for (c) both (a) and (b) (d) none of these

7.10 Which loop is used when number of repetitions are conditional

(a) while (b) for (c) both (a) and (b) (d) none of these

Multiple Choice Questions Answers
7.1 (a), 7.2 (d), 7.3 (b), 7.4 (a), 7.5 (c), 7.6 (a), 7.7 (b), 7.8 (a), 7.9 (b), 7.10 (a)

Short and Long Answer Type Questions

Category I

7.1 Define loop statements. Give a brief about the different types of loop statements.

7.2 Explain for loop with an example.

7.3 Explain nested for loop with an example.

7.4 Compare for loop and while loop with one example of each.

7.5 Explain time functions with an example of each.

7.6 Describe the need for profiling with an example.

Category-II

7.7 Compute the sum of array [1 4 6 7 8] using for loop.

7.8 Evaluate the sum of the square of all numbers from 1 to 10.

7.9 Calculate the sum of the array [1:6, 10, 8] using for loop.

7.10 Find the prime number from 2 to 100 using a nested for loop

7.11 Calculate the summation of all matrix elements $\begin{bmatrix} 4 & 0 & 6 \\ 1 & 5 & 8 \\ 7 & 9 & 5 \end{bmatrix}$ using a nested for loop.

7.12 *Compute the summation of all the matrix elements* $\begin{bmatrix} 4 & 1 & 3 \\ 1 & 2 & 2 \\ 6 & 4 & 0 \end{bmatrix}$ *using a nested for loop.*

7.13 *How many times can 125 be divided by 5 such that the result is less than unity?*

7.14 *Write a program to perform the arithmetic operation for the following type of signals and compute the execution time using timeit function:*
- *(a) time-varying exponential signals*
- *(b) time-varying complex signals*

7.15 *Calculate the total elapsed time while performing element wise multiplication using tic and toc function for the following signals:*
- *(a) time-varying exponential signals*
- *(b) time-varying complex signals*

7.16 *Profile the MATLAB code while performing the arithmetic operation and illustrate the profile summary for the following type of signals:*
- *(c) time-varying exponential signals*
- *(d) time-varying complex signals*

References

[1] 'for loop', 2022 [Online]. Available: https://www.mathworks.com/help/matlab/ref/for.html [Accessed: September-2022].

[2] 'while loop', 2022 [Online]. Available: https://www.mathworks.com/help/matlab/ref/while.html [Accessed: September-2022].

[3] 'Measure the Performance of Your Code', 2022 [Online]. Available: https://www.mathworks.com/help/matlab/matlab_prog/measure-performance-of-your-program.html [Accessed: September-2022].

8 Image Processing and File Handling in MATLAB

UNIT SPECIFICS

This unit covers the following aspects:

- *Basics of image processing in MATLAB*
- *Image enhancement methods*
- *File handling in MATLAB*

This unit first introduces the students to the basics of image processing in MATLAB. Image processing finds applications in various domains, such as intelligent transportation systems, precision agriculture, pervasive computing, ubiquitous computing, etc. MATLAB consists of various tools for image processing. IT Workshop covers the fundamentals of the programming of image processing. This unit then describes the different image enhancement techniques. Such techniques produce the results which help to display a more suitable format and also make them easy for further analysis. It also helps to reduce the time complexity of further image processing. This unit also covers file handling in MATLAB. This unit contains several solved examples of different image processing to develop students' curiosity to explore more about the main content. It consists of many unsolved multiple choice questions and short and long answers type questions. These will help the students to explore new ideas for different applications and develop logical skills. The unit also consists of several references and recommended readings to get more into the theoretical and practical aspects of the main content.

RATIONALE

This unit includes the basics of image processing which includes importing, exporting, and processing the image. It also discusses the displaying method of an image. This unit also covers the image enhancement method. This includes grayscale contrast adjustment and image transformation methods, i.e., linear, logarithmic, and power law transformation methods. This unit also consists of file handling in MATLAB. It exclusively focuses on explaining the concepts with solved examples. This helps students and researchers to apply in practical applications.

PRE-REQUISITES

Basics of MATLAB environment

Basic knowledge of image processing

UNIT OUTCOMES

Following are the outcomes of this unit:

U8-O1: Describe basics of image processing

U8-O2: Apply image enhancement techniques

U8-O3: Illustrate file handling in MATLAB

Unit-8 Outcomes	**EXPECTED MAPPING WITH COURSE OUTCOMES** (1- Weak Correlation; 2- Medium correlation; 3- Strong Correlation)				
	CO-1	**CO-2**	**CO-3**	**CO-4**	**CO-5**
U8-O1	1	-	3	-	2
U8-O2	1	-	1	-	2
U8-O3	1	-	1	-	1

8.1 Introduction to image processing

An image is a 2D function $g(x, y)$, where x and y denote the spatial coordinates. The amplitude on any coordinate x or y represents the intensity of the image. The gray level implies the intensity of monochrome images. The color images comprise red, blue, and green color arrangements, popularly known as the RGB color system.

8.1.1 Importing and displaying an image

MATLAB allows importing the image into the workspace using $imread(\cdot)$ command. It uses $imshow(\cdot)$ command to display the imported image. MATLAB also allows altering the several attributes of an image, e.g., contrast, pixels, etc. The information about any image in the workspace can be extracted using $whos$ command. It provides the information in terms of name, byte, class, and size of the image [1].

SCAN ME
for more about image importing

8.1.2 Write the imported image to another format

MATLAB allows writing the imported image to any other image format using $imwrite(\cdot)$ command. The information can be accessed using $imfinfo(\cdot)$ function.

Example: 8.1

Import an image to MATLAB workspace and convert the image into the grayscale equivalent image. Display the image and its equivalent histogram. Also, extract the information about the image.

Solution:

```
Image1 = imread( 'Original_Image.jpg' );
Image2=rgb2gray(Image1)
figure
imshow (Image2 )
figure
imhist( Image2 )
```

Command Window

```
>>myprog
```

Figure 8.1: *Grayscale equivalent of the original image.*

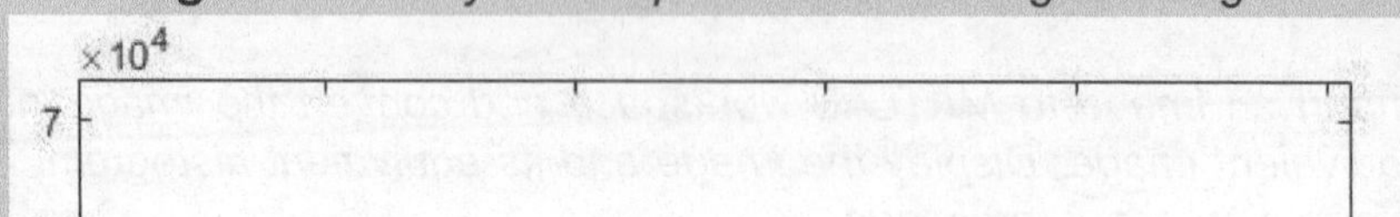

Figure 8.2: *Histogram equivalent of the grayscale image.*

(Continue to change the image file format): *Change the file format of the image in Figure 8.1 and extract the information of the transformed image.*

Solution:

```
I = imread( 'Original_Image.jpg' );
imwrite(I, 'Original_Image.png')
imfinfo('Original_Image.png')
```

Command Window

```
>>myprog
Filename:      'Original_Image.png'
FileModDate: '13-Sep-2022 16:06:39'
FileSize:       2166908
Format:         'png'
Width:          2921
Height:         2057
BitDepth:       8
ColorType:      'grayscale'
ImageModTime: '13 Sep 2022 10:36:38 +0000'
```

8.2 Intensity transformation

MATLAB allows several image processing methods which can enhance the contrast level in an image [2]. These methods adjust the intensity of lower contrast levels and higher contrast levels. Some of the methods are described below:

SCAN ME
for more about image enhancement

8.2.1 Histogram equalization

Histogram equalization spreads the most recurring contrast level. It leads to stretching the image intensity range. It expands the global contrast, and smaller local contrast increases to a higher contrast value. MATLAB uses $imhist(\cdot)$ *function to generate a histogram to check the intensity distribution of an image. It is worth noting that the figure command should be used with* $imhist(\cdot)$ *function in order to avoid overwriting of histogram image over the original image. In MATLAB, users can also enhance the contrast of an image using* $histeq(\cdot)$.

8.2.2 Linear transformation

Linear transformation can be done using two ways, namely:

(a) **Identity transformation:** *When the input image directly maps to the output image, it is said to be an identity transformation method. Thus, the graph between input intensity level and output intensity level is a straight line.*

(b) **Negative transformation:** *In the negative transformation, the input image is negated and mapped onto the output image. Mathematically it is expressed as*

$$I_{Output} = I_{Maximum} - I_{Input} \tag{8.1}$$

where I_{Output} *and* I_{Input} *denote the output and input image intensity.* $I_{Maximum}$ *is the maximum intensity of the grayscale image. If the image is expressed by 8-bit grayscale, then the intensity of the image varies from zero to 255. In negative transformation, each pixel value of the image gets subtracted from 255.*

8.2.3 Logarithmic transformation

In logarithmic transformation, the output image pixels are a logarithmic function of input image pixels. Mathematically it is expressed as

$$I_{Output} = k\,log(I_{Input} + 1) \tag{8.2}$$

where I_{Output} *and* I_{Input} *denote the output and input image pixel values, respectively.* k *is the constant value. This method is based on the fact that higher values of pixels inside the log function get compressed, whereas lower values of the pixels get expanded. One must be added to input pixels inside the log function as it gives the infinite value of output pixel values for zero input pixel values [3].*

8.2.4 Power–law transformation

The power law transformation includes j^{th} *power transformation and* j^{th} *root transformation. Mathematically, it is expressed as*

$$I_{transformed} = k \times I^{\gamma}_{Original} \tag{8.3}$$

where k is the constant. As the transformed image is represented in terms of power (gamma, γ), thus, it is called a gamma transformation. The term γ can be used to obtain the enhanced image [4]. Figure 8.3 shows the input and output intensity levels for different transformation methods.

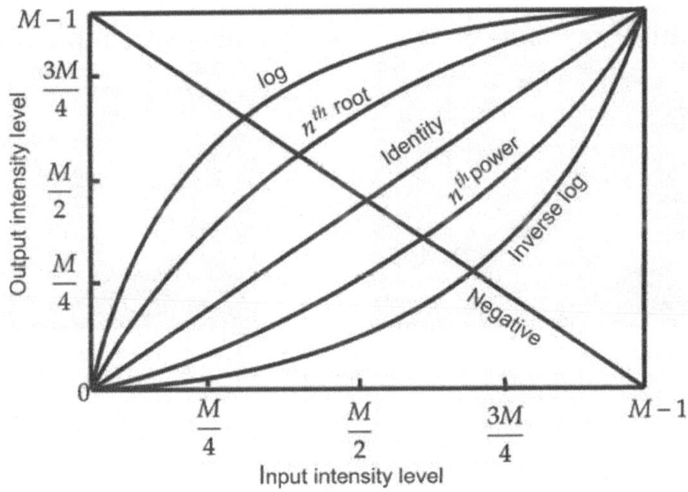

Figure 8.3: *Intensity levels for image transformation methods.*

Example: 8.2

Enhance the contrast of the image using MATLAB. Also, display the histogram of the original and transformed image.

Solution:

```
I1 = imread( 'Original_Image.jpg' );   % Actual image

I2=rgb2gray( I1 );                     % Grayscale image

figure

subplot(2,2,1), imshow( I2)            %Displaying actual grayscale image

title('Actual grayscale image')

I3 = histeq( I2 );                     % Improved contrast image

subplot(2,2,2), imshow( I3 )

title('Image with improved contrast')
```

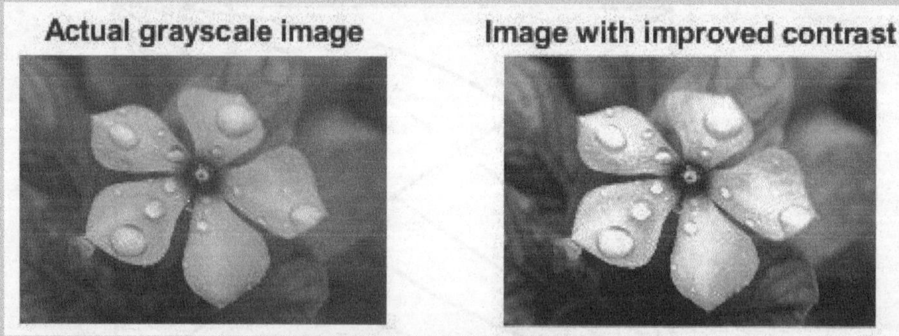

Figure 8.4: *Actual and improved contrast of grayscale image.*

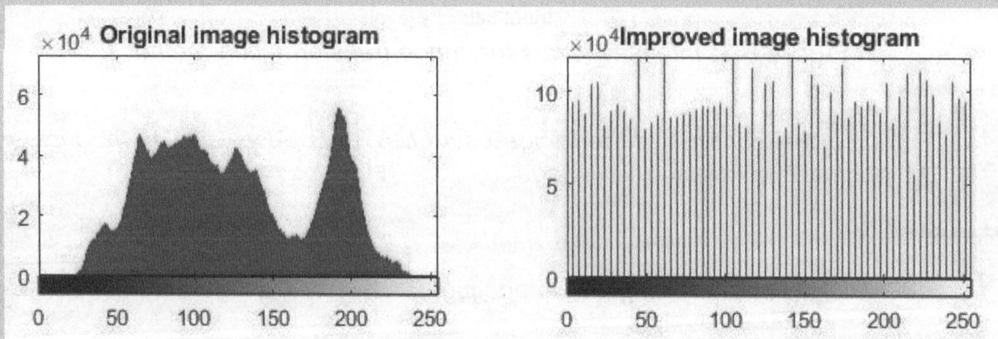

Figure 8.5: *Histogram of the original image and improved contrast image.*

(Continue for negative transformation): *Convert a grayscale image to a negative image.*

Solution:

```
I1 =imread( 'Image2.jpg' );       % Importing actual grayscale image
figure
subplot(2,2,1), imshow(I1)        % Displaying actual image
title('Actual grayscale image')   % Displaying title to actual image
M=256;
I2 = (M - 1) - I1;                % Negative transformed image
subplot(2,2,2), imshow( I2)       %Displaying negative transformed image
title('Negative transformed image')
```

Command Window

```
>>myprog
```

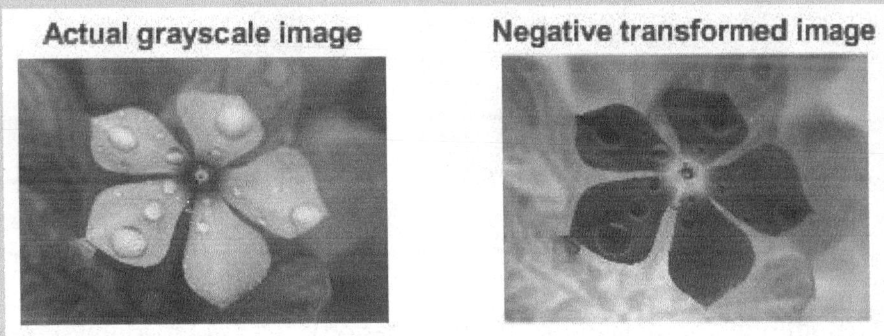

Figure 8.6: *Comparison of the actual and negative transformed image.*

(Continue for logarithmic transformation): *Convert a grayscale image to a logarithmic equivalent.*

Solution:

```
I1 = imread( 'Image2.jpg' );      % Importing actual grayscale image
I2 = im2double(I1);               % Original double  datatype  image
I3 = k * log(I2 + 1);             % Logarithmic transformed image
figure
subplot(2,2,1), imshow(I1)     % Displaying actual grayscale image
title ('Actual grayscale image')
subplot(2,2,2), imshow( I3)    % Displaying logarithmic transformed image
title( 'Logarithmic transformed image' )
```

Command Window

```
>>myprog
```

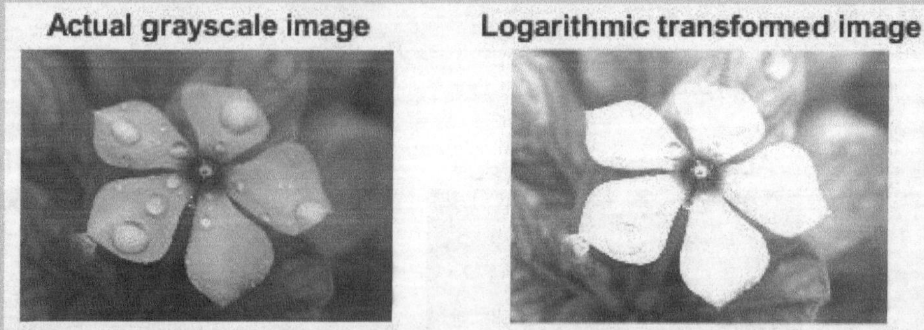

Figure 8.7: *Comparison of the actual and logarithmic transformed image.*

(Continue for power law transformation): *Transform a grayscale image using the power law transformation method.*

Solution:

```
Image1= imread('Image2.jpg');   % Actual grayscale image
Image2 = im2double( I1 )    % Grayscale image to double data type image
subplot(2,2,1), imshow(Image1);     %Displaying actual grayscale image
title( 'Actual grayscale image' )
Transformed_Image1 = 2*(Image2.^0.75);
subplot(2,2,2), imshow( Transformed_Image1 );
title( 'Transformed image ( \gamma = 0.75)' )
Transformed_Image2 = 2*(Image2.^1.25);
subplot(2,2,3), imshow( Transformed_Image2 );
title( 'Transformed image (\gamma = 1.25)' )
Transformed_Image3 = 2*(Image2.^1.50);
subplot(2,2,4), imshow(Transformed_Image3);
title( 'Transformed image (\gamma = 1.50)' )
```

Results

Command Window
>>myprog

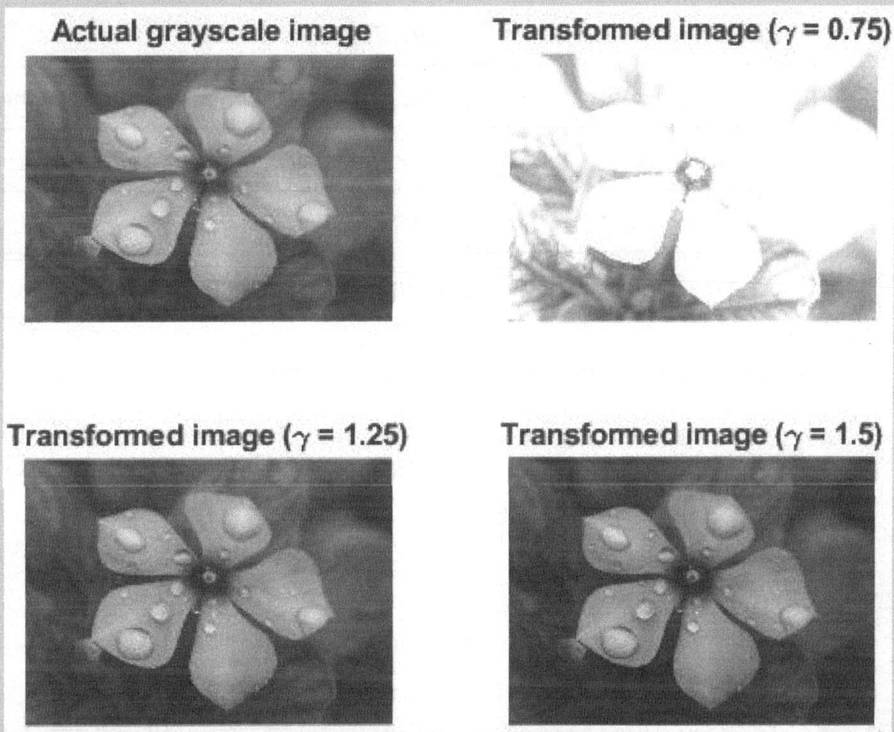

Figure: 8.8: *Power law transformation of the image.*

8.3 File handling in MATLAB

File handling includes exporting the data to text files that have low-level input-output. It involves combining the numerical value and character data appended with non-rectangular files. For this purpose, it uses $fprintf$ *function, which is a vector version that can write data from an array [5]. Syntax for* $fprintf$ *is*

SCAN ME for more about file handling in MATLAB

$$fprintf(fileID, formatSpec, X1, X2,..., Xn)$$

- **Opening a file:** $fopen(\cdot)$ *can be used to open the file. The file can be accessed in read-only mode. Thus, users need to define the permission by writing 'w', 'a', etc. It generates a file identifier when* $fopen(\cdot)$ *is used.*

- **Writing to a file:** *It uses several specifiers or symbols to print values. Table 8.1 shows the specifiers which are used to print the different values.*

Table 8.1: *Specifiers or symbols with their specifications.*

Specifiers or symbols	Specification
\n or \r\n	*This represents proceed to a new line*
%f	*This specifier is used to print floating-point numbers*
%d	*It denotes integer values*
%s	*It prints the character values*

- *It uses $fclose(\cdot)$ function to close the file after finishing.*

Example: 8.3

Prepare a table for the expression $t\sin(4\pi t)$ and save to a file Sinusoidaltable.txt.

Solution:

```
t = 0 : 0.01 : 0.1;                 % Define time series
z = [t; t.*sin(4*pi*t)];            % Define the mathematical expression
fileID = fopen('Sinusoidaltable.txt','w'); % Open the file
fprintf(fileID, 'Mathematical expression\n\n');
fprintf(fileID,'%f %f\n', z);
fclose(fileID);                      % Close the file
```

Command Window

```
>> type Sinusoidaltable.txt
Mathematical expression
0.000000    0.000000
0.010000    0.001253
0.020000    0.004974
0.030000    0.011044
0.040000    0.019270
0.050000    0.029389
0.060000    0.041073
0.070000    0.053936
```

0.080000	0.067546
0.090000	0.081434
0.100000	0.095106

UNIT SUMMARY

- *Image enhancement includes*
  - *Histogram equalization*
  - *Linear transformation*
    - *(a) Identity transformation*
    - *(b) Negative transformation*
  - *Logarithmic transformation*
  - *Power law transformation*
- *File handling includes exporting the data to text files which have low-level input-output.*

EXERCISES

Multiple Choice Questions

8.1 Which of the following function is used to import the image

(a) $imread(\cdot)$ *(b)* $imageread(\cdot)$ *(c)* $readim(\cdot)$ *(d) none of these*

8.2 Which of the following function is used display the histogram of an image

(a) $histimage(\cdot)$ *(b)* $histim(\cdot)$ *(c)* $imhist(\cdot)$ *(d) none of these*

8.3 Consider I_{Input} *denotes the output and input image intensity.* $I_{Maximum}$ *is the maximum intensity of the grayscale image. Then, the correct expression for negative transformation is*

(a) $I_{Maximum} - I_{Input}$ *(b)* $I_{Minimum} - I_{Input}$ *(c)* $I_{Minimum} + I_{Input}$ *(d)* $I_{Maximum} + I_{Input}$

8.4 Consider $I_{Original}$ denotes the original image intensity and γ is the constant value. The correct expression for power law transformation is

(a) $k \times I_{Original}$ *(b)* $k \times I^{\gamma}_{Original}$ *(c)* $k \times \gamma \times I^{\gamma}_{Original}$ *(d) none of these*

8.5 Consider I_{Input} denotes the input image intensity. The correct expression for logarithmic transformation is

(a) $k\, log(I_{Input} + 1)$ *(b)* $k\, log(I_{Input})$ *(c)* $log(\, log(I_{Input} + 1))$ *(d) none of these*

8.6 Which symbol is is used to print floating-point numbers

(a) \f (b) %d (c) %n (d) %f

8.7 Which symbol is is used to print integer numbers

(a) %d (b) %n (c) %i (d) %f

8.8 Which symbol is is used to print character values

(a) %d (b) %n (c) %c (d) %s

Multiple Choice Questions Answers
8.1 (a), 8.2 (c), 8.3 (a), 8.4 (b), 8.5 (a), 8.6 (d), 8.7 (a), 8.8 (d)

Short and Long Answer Type Questions

8.1 *Explain the importing and displaying an image with an example.*

8.2 *Explain the histogram equalization with an example.*

8.3 *Describe the grayscale transformation methods*

8.4 *Explain the following with an example*
- *(a) Identity transformation*
- *(b) Negative transformation*

8.5 *Describe the following with an example*
  (c) *Logarithmic transformation*
  (d) *Power law transformation*

8.6 *Describe the file handling with an example.*

8.7 *Prepare a table for the expression* $t^2 cos(5\pi t)$ *and save to a file Mathematicaltable.txt.*

PRACTICAL

Experiment 8.1: Extract features of an image using MATLAB.

Aim

Find the features of an image using MATLAB.

Apparatus

MATLAB

Theory

The attributes of an image are defined in terms of width, height, class, and image type. MATLAB uses $imattributes(\cdot)$ *for this purpose.*

MATLAB simulation

```
clc
clear all
close all
Image = imshow('Image1.jpg');
Attributes = imattributes(Image)
```

Results

Command Window
>>myprog

Figure 8.9: *Original image considered for obtaining attributes.*

Attributes =

4×2 cell array

{ 'Width (columns)' }   {'775' }

{ 'Height (rows)' }   {'557' }

{ 'Class' }   {'uint8' }

{ 'Image type' }   { 'truecolor' }

Conclusions

This experiment explains the attributes and method to find the attributes of an image. Initially the user need to import the image from the memory drive to MATLAB program by giving the proper path to the image. Then, the attributes are obtained using `imattributes` $(\cdot)$ *command.*

Experiment 8.2: MATLAB program for image negation.

Aim

Design a MATLAB program for obtaining a negative image.

Apparatus

MATLAB

Theory

The negative image transformation is the linear transformation of an image. It can be used to detect the various information of an image. It has been widely used by archeologists and biomedical researchers, etc. In the image negation, the input image is negated and maps onto the resultant image.

MATLAB simulation

```
Image1=imread( 'Image1.jpg' );          % Import the actual image
Image2=rgb2gray(Image1);                % Actual grayscale image
figure
subplot(2,2,1), imshow(Image2);         %Displaying actual grayscale image
M=256;
Image3=(M-1) - Image2;                  %Negative transformed image
subplot(2,2,2), imshow(Image3)          %Displaying negative transformed image
```

Results

Command Window

```
>>myprog
```

Original image

Negative transformed image

Figure: 8.10: *Comparison of original and negative transformed image.*

Conclusions

This experiment demonstrates image negation using MATLAB. Initially, it imports the original image using $imread(\cdot)$ *command. Then, it does the image negation of the original image.*

Experiment 8.3: MATLAB program for power law transformation.

Aim

Design a MATLAB program to perform power law transformation of an image.

Apparatus

MATLAB

Theory

The transformed image using power law transformation is expressed as

$$I_{Transformed} = k \times I^{\gamma}_{Original}$$

where k is the constant. As the transformed image is represented in terms of power (gamma, γ), thus, it is called as gamma transformation. The term γ can be used to obtain the enhanced image.

MATLAB simulation

```
I = imread('Image2.jpg');                  %Import actual grayscale image
Image_double=im2double(I)
subplot(2,2,1), imshow(I);        % Plotting actual grayscale image
title('Actual greyscale image')
Transformed_Image1 = 2*(Image_double.^0.75);
subplot(2,2,2), imshow(Transformed_Image1); %Plotting transformed image(γ =0.75)
title('Transformed image (\gamma = 0.75)')
Transformed_Image2 = 2*(Image_double.^1.25);
subplot(2,2,3), imshow(Transformed_Image2); %Plotting transformed image(γ =1.25)
title('Transformed image (\gamma = 1.25)')
Transformed_Image3 = 2*(Image_double.^1.50);
subplot(2,2,4), imshow(Transformed_Image3); %Plotting transformed image(γ =1.5)
title('Transformed image (\gamma = 1.5)')
```

Results

Command Window

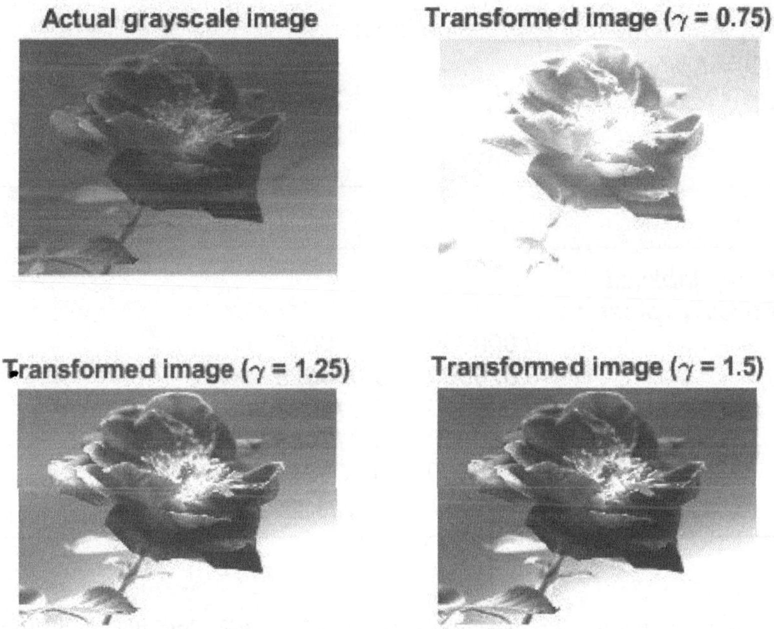

Figure: 8.11: *Image transformation using power law transformation method.*

Conclusions

This experiment demonstrates the power law transformation of an image using MATLAB. Initially, it imports the original image using $imread(\cdot)$ *command. Then, it does the image transformation of the image using different values of parameter* γ.

Experiment 8.4: File handling in MATLAB

Aim

Illustrate a file handling program using MATLAB for a mathematical expression.

Apparatus

MATLAB

Theory

File handling exports the data to text files that have low-level input-output. It involves combining the numerical value and character data appended with non-rectangular files.

MATLAB simulation

```
t = 0 : 0.02 : 0.1;
z = [t; t.*cos(6*pi*t).*sin(4*pi*t)];
```

```
fileID = fopen('Trigotable.txt','w');
fprintf(fileID, 'Mathematical expression\n\n');
fprintf(fileID,'%f %f\n', z);
fclose(fileID);
```

Results

Command Window
>> type Trigotable.txt *Mathematical expression* 0.000000 0.000000 0.020000 0.004625 0.040000 0.014047 0.060000 0.017488 0.080000 0.004241 0.100000 -0.029389

Conclusions

This experiment demonstrates the file handling in MATLAB. Initially, it opens the file using $fopen(\cdot)$ command. Then, it prints the character 'Mathematical expression'. It also prints the numerical values of the mathematical expression after computation.

References

[1] 'Basic Image Import', 2022 [Online]. Available: https://www.mathworks.com/help/images/image-import-and-export.html [Accessed: September-2022].

[2] Gonzalez, Rafael C. Digital image processing. Pearson Education India, 2009.

[3] 'Log Transform', 2022 [Online]. Available: https://www.mathworks.com/matlabcentral/fileexchange/50286-log-transform [Accessed: September-2022].

[4] 'Power law transformation', 2022 [Online]. Available: https://www.mathworks.com/matlabcentral/fileexchange/56934-power-law-transformation-of-an-image [Accessed: September-2022].

[5] 'Export to Text Data Files', 2022 [Online]. Available: https://www.mathworks.com/help/matlab/import_export/writing-to-text-data-files-with-low-level-io.html [Accessed: September-2022].

9 MATLAB Program Organization and Debugging Techniques

UNIT SPECIFICS

This unit covers the following aspects:

- *MATLAB program organization*
- *Menu-driven modular program*
- *Debugging techniques*
- *SCILAB programming*

This unit familiarizes the students with MATLAB program organization. It then discusses the menu-driven modular program which takes the inputs and displays the output in terms of user choices. This unit also covers debugging techniques which help in removing errors in the program statements. It also contains an introduction to SCILAB programming.

The unit consists of several solved examples to develop the student's curiosity to apply in ongoing research applications. This unit consists of many unsolved multiple choice questions and short and long answers type questions. These will help the students to explore new ideas for different applications. The unit also consists of several references and recommended readings which help students to explore more theoretical and practical aspects of the main content.

RATIONALE

This unit covers MATLAB program organization that leads to improvement in the readability of the program statement. It uses a cell folding method for this purpose. It also comprises the application of menu-driven modular programming. It gives the user's choice outputs in the form of several options for a given input. This unit also consists of various debugging techniques that help the users locate the error in the program statement to remove errors. Besides these, it also covers the introduction to SCI programming. For developing the student's curiosity and understanding of the main content, this contains solved examples to explain the content for practical implementation.

PRE-REQUISITES

Basics of MATLAB environment

Operation with functions, loops, and branching statements

Basic knowledge of linear algebra

UNIT OUTCOMES

List of outcomes of this unit is as follows:

U9-O1: Describe MATLAB program organization

U9-O2: Apply menu-driven modular programming

U9-O3: Illustrate debugging techniques

U9-O4: Introduce SCILAB programming

Unit-9 Outcomes	EXPECTED MAPPING WITH COURSE OUTCOMES (1- Weak Correlation; 2- Medium correlation; 3- Strong Correlation)				
	CO-1	CO-2	CO-3	CO-4	CO-5
U9-O1	1	-	-	-	3
U9-O2	1	-	-	-	3
U9-O3	1	-	-	-	3
U9-O4	1	-	-	-	3

9.1 MATLAB program organization

MATLAB program organization is an important technique to improve the readability of the programs. The cell folding method is a widely used method for this purpose. It allows users to fold the program lines for long and complex programs [1]. In this method, the user must turn on the code folding using the following way

$$Preferences \rightarrow Editor/Debugger \rightarrow Code\ Folding.$$

Following steps need to perform for code folding:

Step 1: *The cell marker (%%) should be inserted to the raw code such that the folded part of the code must be within the cell marker. After applying the cell marker, the folded part of the program code is confined to a rectangular strip. This is illustrated in Figure 9.1.*

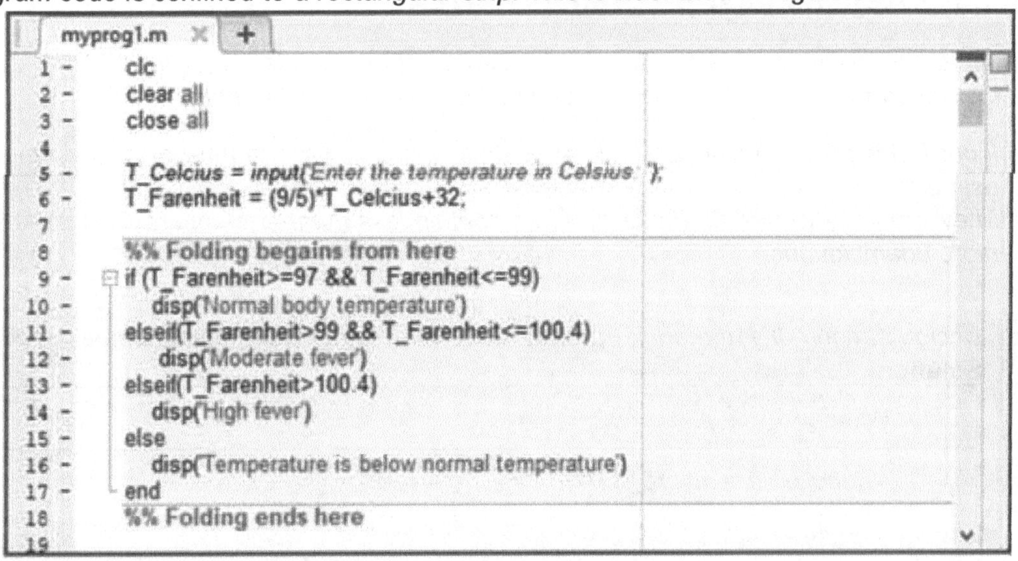

Figure 9.1: *Cell marker insertion in cell folding method.*

Step 2: *In the second step, the user can minimize the chunk of the code by right-clicking the cursor and selecting '$Code\ Folding \rightarrow Fold\ All$'. Alternatively, users can use $Ctrl + \ =$ to minimize the selected chunk of the code. Figure 9.2 shows the minimized code. The users can again maximize the chunk of the code by clicking on the three dots displayed in the minimized code chunk.*

Following are the merits of program organization:

- *It becomes useful for long program statements, where debugging becomes easy after the proper organization of the program.*
- *The separation of the program statements is advantageous as it reduces the complexity of the program.*
- *The users can also store the data in a different folder and call the program if required.*

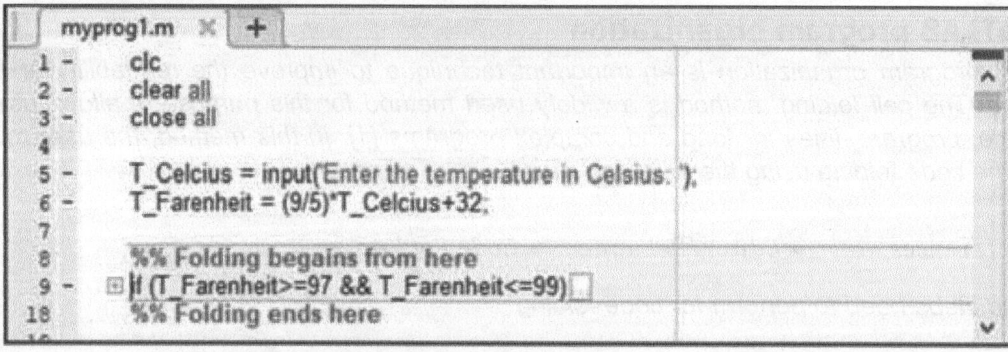

Figure 9.2: *Minimized program after cell folding method.*

9.2 Menu-driven modular program in MATLAB

A modular-driven program gets the input and displays the choices through which the user selects the preferable option. It consists of several merits as described below:

1) *Input is introduced using a single key; thus, there is less chance of error from the user side.*
2) *They are easy to use as these systems contain less number of inputs. This makes it more unambiguous.*

Example: 9.1

Design a menu-driven modular program to enter the details of the students.

Solution:

Editor Window 1

```
function n = myprog11(x)
while true
   n=str2double(input(x, 's'));
   if ~isnan(n)
      break;
   end
end
```

Editor Window 2

```
function output1 = MyComponent( input1 )
for j = 1:length( input1 )
```

```
   fprintf('%d, %s\n', j, input1{ j });
end
output1 = 0;
while ~any( output1 == 1 : length( input1 ))
   output1 = myprog11( 'Select the option: ' );
end
```

Editor Window 3

```
StudentDetails = {'Student Name', 'Branch Name', 'Exit'};
name = '';
while true
   out1 = MyComponent(StudentDetails);
   if out1 == 1
      name = input('Student name: ', 's');
   elseif out1 == 2
      name = input('Branch name: ', 's');
   elseif out1 == 3
      break;
   end
end
```

Command Window

```
>>studentdetail
1, Student Name
2, Branch Name
3, Exit
Select the option: 1
Student name: Ram
```

```
1, Student Name
2, Branch Name
3, Exit
Select the option: 2
Branch name: Computer Science and Engineering

1, Student Name
2, Branch Name
3, Exit
Select the option: 3
>>
```

Description of Example 9.1: *This example illustrates the menu driven modular program to display the student's name or branch, which depends on the option that students choose. Initially, it uses the function myprog11 in the first editor window to enter only the valid number to select the option; otherwise, it will ask to enter a valid number to enter again. In the second editor window, MyComponent function displays the menu of the option through which the student needs to select the option. In the third editor window, it defines the menu items i.e., Student Name, Branch Name, Exit. When executing the program in the command window, it first displays the menu items. If the student selects the first option, then it asks the student to enter the student's name. Similarly, if the student selects the second option, then it asks the student to enter the branch name. Choosing the third option leads to the exit of the program.*

Generating multiple option dialog boxes: *MATLAB contains an inbuilt function to create multiple choice boxes, which can be used for different applications [2]. The syntax for generating multiple boxes is given below*

SCAN ME
for more about menu

$$choice = menu(message, options)$$

Here, the inbuilt MATLAB function $menu(\cdot)$ *generates the multiple option boxes, so that user can select any one of the options available.*

Example: 9.2

Design a system that takes the input of several color options and plot the graph using the same color.

Solution:

```
Option = menu("Opt a color","Yellow","Blue","Red", "Green", "Black")
colors = ["y" "b" "r" "g" "k"];
```

```
PlotColor = colors(Option);
t = 0 : 0.01 : 10;
Signal = exp(-0.25*t) .* cos(6*pi*t);
plot(t,Signal,PlotColor, 'LineWidth', 2)
xlabel('Time');
ylabel('Amplitude');
```

Command Window

```
>> myprogram
```

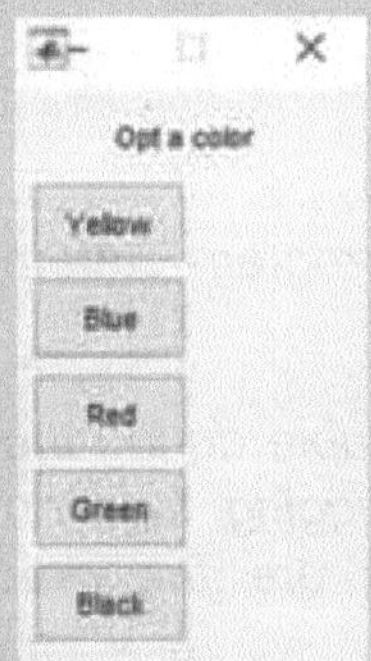

Figure 9.3: *Options available to select any one of the given choices.*

```
Option =
     2
```

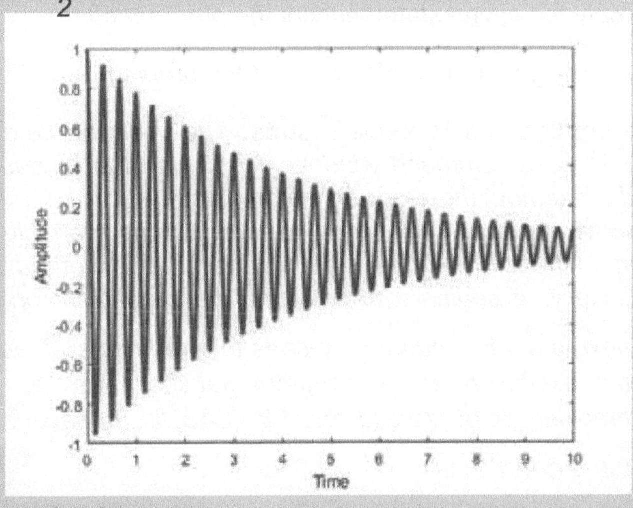

Figure 9.4: *Illustration of plotting of the graph in MATLAB.*

Description of Example 9.2: *This example explains the application of* $menu(\cdot)$ *function in MATLAB. Initially, it generates the message as 'Opt a color', and options as 'Yellow, Blue, Red, Green, Black' using the menu function as shown in Figure 9.3. A new window is popup that displays the available color options. After selecting the option, it will select the same color in plotting the waveform as shown in Figure 9.4.*

9.3 Debugging techniques

SCAN ME
for more about debugging

MATLAB programs can have errors in the program statement, which yields unexpected output. These errors can be classified as

Syntax errors *because of misspelling or incorrect way of writing MATLAB keywords. Incorrect punctuation also results in syntax errors.*

Runtime errors *are caused due to invalid loop arrays. These loop arrays sometimes result in infinite loops.*

Logical errors *occur when program statements have invalid operators, resulting in wrong output.*

The users can identify the trouble during the execution of the program using the debugging techniques. It uses the debugging function that can be used in the editor window or command window. Following are the precautions that must be taken before applying debugging techniques:

I. **Save editor fle:** *The users must save the program file before executing in debugging form.*
II. **Command window execution:** *If a file is not completely saved, then MATLAB will execute only the saved statements of the program code.*

Following are the debugging methods to detect the problem:

I. **Remove semicolons to show results:** *The user can detect the issue by displaying the output in the command window. To display the output, the semicolons must be removed throughout the program statements.*
II. **'*Breakpoint*' button:** *This method checks the variable status in the program statements. The following steps are involved in this method:*
    (a) *Initially, it begins with selecting the breakpoint on the dashed line which is next to the line number. It leads to a red circle to appear. At the red circle, the execution of the program pauses. This red circle indicates that the breaking point is valid and MATLAB file is saved. If the file is not saved, it turns gray .*
    (b) *If the code is executed, then a green arrow appears, which means that the marked statement has not been executed yet. To check the line, Run next*

line  button is used. It continues for the entire program until it shows the error in the command window.

(c) *The users can use the Continue  to detect the next breakpoint.*

(d) *Once the error is detected, the debugging can be quit using Debugging Quit  button.*

III. **Check variable value:** *The users can also check the variable value for debugging. For this method, the cursor should be moved over the variable to display the variable value. If there is any error, it will not show the variable value. This is illustrated in Figure 9.5.*

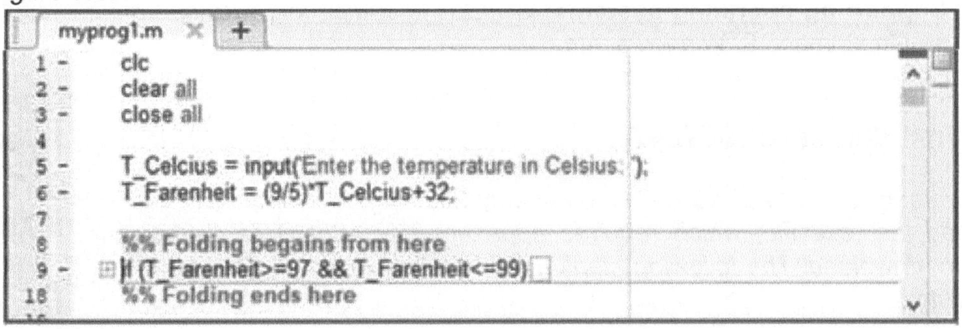

Figure 9.5: *Illustration of checking the variable value in the editor window.*

The users can also check the variable value by typing the variable in the command window.

IV. *MATLAB also allows pausing the long executing program statements. For pausing the code, the user should click on Pause button . After correcting the issue, the program can be continued using Continue button .*

9.4 SCILAB Programming

SCILAB is abbreviated from the word 'Scientific Laboratory'. This is a freely available programming language that operates analogously to MATLAB. It is written in C, C++, Java, Fortran and the official website is https://www.scilab.org/. It was developed by the researchers from ENPC and INRIA in 1990. Since 2012, SCILAB has been maintained and developed by the ESI group [4].

SCAN ME
for more about SCILAB

9.4.1 Features of SCILAB

Following are the key features of SCILAB [5]:

I. **Solution to the mathematical equation:** *SCILAB allows the user to solve mathematical equations e.g., ordinary differential equations, differential algebraic equations etc. It has a large number of mathematical functions to accomplish the task.*
II. **Helps in developing complex algorithms:** *SCILAB can help the researchers to develop the complex algorithms. It is a high programming language that consists of a wide range of numerical and programming functions.*
III. **Graphical representation:** *SCILAB allows the users to display the output in graphical representation, bar graphs, MathML annotations, etc. These output representations help the users to visualize the results in a better way.*
IV. **Supporting operating systems:** *SCILAB is compatible with operating systems such as Linux, macOS, Windows, etc.*

9.4.2 Installation of SCILAB

SCAN ME
for more about downloading SCILAB

Latest version of SCILAB was released in July 2021 [6]. The users need to download the .exe file, which requires approximately 168MB of memory space to download. The following steps need to follow to install SCILAB on a computer:

- *The user needs to run the .exe file and agree to make the changes when it asks for license agreement between the user and ESI group. It is mandatory to accept the agreement; otherwise, it is not possible to install the SCILAB.*
- *After the installation, the user can finish the installation, and it is ready to use.*

Unit Summary

- *MATLAB program organization improves the readability of the program statements.*
- *Cell folding method is a widely used method for MATLAB program organization.*
- *A modular-driven program takes the input from the user and displays the preferable options.*
- *Debugging techniques help in the detection and correction of the trouble in the program statements. The errors that generally occur are*
  - *syntax error*
  - *logical error*
  - *runtime error*
- *Debugging techniques include*

- *Remove semicolons to show results*
- *'Breakpoint' button*
- *Check variable value*

- *SCILAB is a freely available programming language that operates analogously to MATLAB.*

EXERCISES

Multiple Choice Questions

9.1 In the cell folding method, which symbol is used as a cell marker?

(a) %% *(b) $$* *(c) @@* *(d) ##*

9.2 In cell folding method, which shortcut is used to minimize the selected chunk of the code

(a) $Ctrl + -$ *(b)* $Ctrl + =$ *(c)* $Ctrl + /$ *(d)* $Ctrl + |$

9.3 Menu driven modular program contains__________number of inputs.

(a) more *(b) less* *(c) both (a) and (b)* *(d) None of these*

9.4 Consider the following program statement

```
Option = menu("Opt a color","Option 1","Option 2","Option 3", "Option 4")
colors = ["r" "b" "g" "k"];
PlotColor = colors(Option);
t = 0 : 0.01 : 10;
Signal = cos(6*pi*t);
plot(t,Signal,PlotColor, 'LineWidth', 2)
xlabel('Time');
ylabel('Amplitude');
```

Select the correct option after opting 'Option 2'

(a) *(b)* *(c)* *(d)*

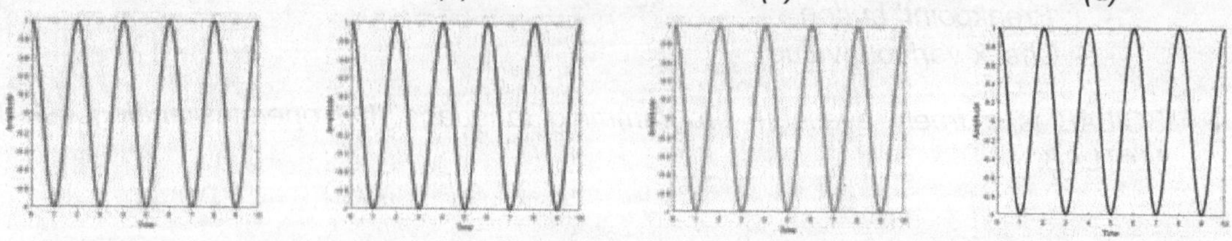

9.5 Which of the following is correct sequence after executing following program statement

Options = menu("Opt a color","Red","Blue", "Green", "Black")

(a)

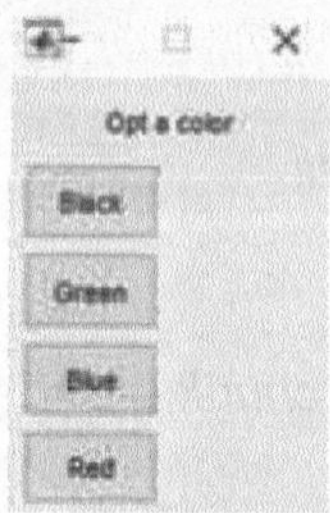

(b)

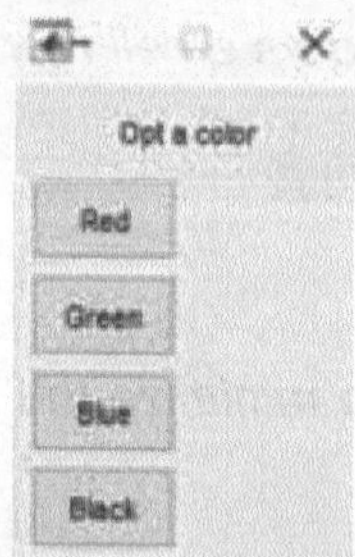

(c)

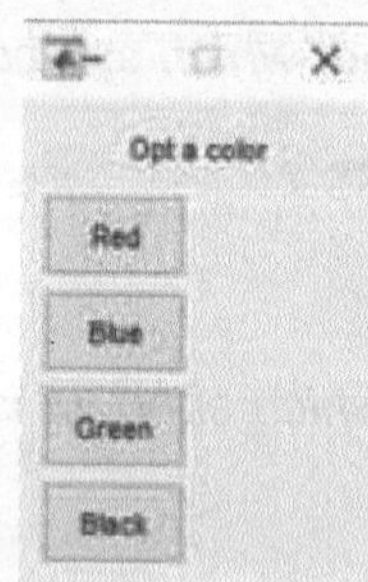

(d) None of these

9.6 Statement 1: Runtime errors are caused due to invalid loop arrays.
Statement 2: Incorrect punctuation also leads to runtime errors.

(a) Statement 1 is correct *(b) Statement 2 is correct* *(c) Both Statements are correct* *(d) None of these*

9.7 Statement 1: Logical errors are caused due to invalid loop arrays.
Statement 2: Incorrect punctuation also leads to logical errors.

(a) Statement 1 is correct *(b) Statement 2 is correct* *(c) Both Statements are correct* *(d) None of these*

9.8 The word SCILAB is the abbreviated name of

(a) Science LAB *(b) Science Laboratory* *(c) Scientific Laboratory* *(d) Scientific Lab*

9.9 In which language SCILAB is written?

(a) C, C++, Java, Fortran. (b) C, C++, Java (c) C, C++, Fortran (d) Java, Fortran

9.10 SCILAB was developed in

(a) 1995 (b) 2000 (c) 1992 (d) 1990

9.11 Which of the following operating system (s) support SCILAB

(a) Linux and macOS (b) macOS and Windows (c) Windows (d) Linux, macOS, and Windows

Multiple Choice Questions Answers
9.1 (a), 9.2 (b), 9.3 (b), 9.4 (b), 9.5 (c), 9.6 (a), 9.7 (d), 9.8 (c), 9.9 (a), 9.10 (d), 9.11 (d)

Short and Long Answer Type Questions

Category I

9.1 What is program organization in MATLAB? Explain with an example.

9.2 Explain the cell folding method with a suitable example.

9.3 Enlist the merits and demerits of program organization in MATLAB.

9.4 Describe the menu driven modular program. What are the merits of such a modular program?

9.5 How to generate a multiple option dialog box? Explain with one application.

9.6 What is needed for debugging? What are the precautions that must be taken before applying debugging techniques?

9.7 Explain the errors in the program statement that leads to unexpected output.

9.8 Describe the different debugging methods for detecting the error in program statements.

9.9 Explain the debugging using the 'Breakpoint' button with an example.

9.10 Write a short note on SCILAB. What are the key features of SCILAB?

Category-II

9.11 *Design a system that displays the following city name 'Delhi, Chennai, Kolkata, Mumbai' as a menu for other applications.*

9.12 *Design a system that takes the input of several color options and plots the graph of the system $y = x(t)cos(4\pi t)$ using the selected color.*

References

[1] *'How to organize your code in blocks', 2022 [Online]. Available: https://www.mathworks.com/matlabcentral/answers/23538-how-to-organize-your-code-in-blocks [Accessed: September-2022].*

[2] *'Menu', 2022 [Online]. Available: https://www.mathworks.com/help/matlab/ref/menu.html [Accessed: September-2022].*

[3] *'Debug MATLAB Code Files', 2022 [Online]. Available: https://www.mathworks.com/help/matlab/matlab_prog/debugging-process-and-features.html [Accessed: September-2022].*

[4] *'About SCILAB', 2022 [Online]. Available: https://www.mathworks.com/help/matlab/matlab_prog/debugging-process-and-features.html [Accessed: September-2022].*

[5] *'Features of SCILAB', 2022 [Online]. Available: https://www.scilab.org/about [Accessed: September-2022].*

[6] *'SCILAB download link', 2022 [Online]. Available: https://www.scilab.org/download/scilab-6.1.1 [Accessed: September-2022].*